The Color of Racism:

Understanding & Overcoming Discrimination

D1709950

The Color of Racism is available at special quantity discounts for bulk purchases for sales promotions, premiums, fund raising or educational use. Special books or book excerpts can also be created to fit special needs.

For details write to Transformax International, Special Marketing Department, 701 Loyola Avenue, P.O. Box 53082, New Orleans, Louisiana 70153-3082.

The Color of Racism:

Understanding & Overcoming Discrimination

Sam B. Pearson, III

A Transformax Book
Published by Transformax International
New Orleans

701 Loyola Avenue
P.O. Box 53082
New Orleans, Louisiana 70153-3082

Publisher: Transformax International
Editor: Donna G. Fricke, Ph.D.
Proofreaders: Kimberly Thibeaux, Patricia
Pettifoot, Tonya Armbruster
Interior Design: Maria Burke
Front Cover: Perryn Waelde
Printer and Binder: Gilliland Printing

Copyright © 1995 by Transformax International
Second Printing, 1996
Third Printing, 1996

For information address Transformax International,
701 Loyola Avenue
P.O. Box 53082
New Orleans, Louisiana 70153-3082

Library of Congress Catalog Card Number: 95-61793

ISBN: 0-9650220-0-5

Printed in the U.S.A.

Dedication:

To all the people whose sacrifices gave African-Americans opportunities to be successful today

Acknowledgements

My concern about the devastating effects of racism on African-Americans prompted me to write this book. Taking *The Color of Racism* from conception to completion was challenging; however, many people helped me to transform my ideas into a reality. I now wish to acknowledge those very special people for their contributions:

Donna G. Fricke, Ph.D., Director of Graduate Studies and Research, Maine Maritime Academy, who edited the manuscript. Thanks, Donna. You did a great job.

Kimberly M. Thibeaux, graduate student at Tulane University, who found time between her classes, studies and work to proofread the original draft. Thanks, Kim. Your feedback was practical.

Patricia Pettifoot, librarian, Jefferson Parish Library, who also proofread the original draft. Thanks, Pat, your feedback was encouraging.

Tonya Armbruster, Marine License Consultant, and Business major at the University of New Orleans, who carefully went through the final draft to ascertain that it was ready for typesetting. Thanks, Tonya.

Maria Burke, owner and operator of *Professional Images*, who designed the pages and back cover. Thanks, Maria.

Thanks to the staff at TLC Printing, especially **Kris** and **Perryn**, who offered me valuable printing suggestions. **Larry,** you've got a great team.

To order autographed copies of *The Color of Racism*, see last page.

Table of Contents

Introduction

What color would you have chosen to be if you had the choice before birth? What if there were a "chameleo-surgery" procedure that could simply change your color? Would racism have affected your decision? Would you be a lot happier if you were not black? Think about it.

Unfortunately, being black can be very frustrating. Racism is everywhere: in the newspapers, on television, radio, the streets, parks, schools, offices, and even in churches. There are often implications—sometimes subtle, sometimes bold—that blacks are inferior, bad, thieves, lazy, not intelligent or not good enough. We have all experienced this to some extent.

Fortunately, the problem is not being black. Many recognize that African-Americans have made extraordinary advancements in various areas—entertainment, sports, the military, education, politics, medicine, and even the aerospace industry, for example. Blacks have certainly proven themselves capable. Besides, African-Americans are not the only ones who are discriminated against. Jews, Native Americans, Hispanics, and other ethnic groups have their share of discrimination too.

Skin color is simply not the problem. The problem is racism. It's about control. It's about trying to feel superior by making someone else feel inferior. It's about the way people allow the monster of racism to affect them. However, racism, like any other problem, has a solution. And that solution is what this book is all about.

There is no longer any need to regret being born black, running away from yourself, being ashamed of your color, fearing racism, pretending racism doesn't exist, living and dying in poverty, hurting your loved ones, or destroying yourself because of the effects of racism. This book can help solve the problem.

The purpose of this book is not to investigate the history of racism or to blame anyone. The damage is done, but that's not the end of the story. This book is designed to help you understand the truth about racism, what it can and cannot do. And second, to enable you to develop criteria that will make you successful at whatever you choose. This book will give you the necessary knowledge to have power over racism. When you are in control, your self-confidence will increase; you will be able to achieve a lot more. Racism will not be able to tell you that you can't, because you will know better. Racism will no longer have the power to frustrate, hurt, or frighten you.

You do not have the option of changing your skin color. Even if you did, you probably wouldn't want to do so after reading this book. Nevertheless, you do have a choice of not allowing racism to predict and control your life. You can be as great as you want to be. You can be an outstanding role model. The possibilities are virtually endless; you set your own limits. The power to do it all is now in your hands. Read on to discover how to take control of success in your life.

Laws cannot stop discrimination, but attitudes can.

WE MUST OVERCOME RACISM

BANG! The loud noise startled Lichelle. She instinctively reached for her heart, as the half-peeled potato fell out of her hands. She gave a sign of relief when she heard little footsteps racing upstairs. It had only been the front door slamming. Her heart was still pounding furiously when she called out, "Keith, is that you?"

"Yea, Ma," a soft, depressed voice replied. She sensed that something was wrong. Walking towards the stairs, she asked if everything was all right. "Everything's fine, Ma," Keith replied. His voice was a poor imitation of his usual cheery tone. Stopping halfway up the flight of stairs, he was careful not to turn as his mother walked up. He didn't want her to see that he had been crying. He wasn't aware that his voice had already betrayed him.

When Lichelle reached Keith, she knelt on the step behind him. She held his shoulder and gently turned him around to face her. Keith was trembling. Lichelle had never seen him like this before. Whatever was bothering him had to be serious.

Keith and his mother were close. They had only each other. He never knew his father who was serving time for drug trafficking. Shortly before Keith's father was incarcerated, he had beaten Lichelle mercilessly. She went into early labor.

Keith's premature birth was a turning point for Lichelle. She became determined to make the best of her life; an innocent child was now looking up to her. When Keith was old enough to go to day-care, Lichelle went back to finish high school. She later went to college and graduated magna cum laude with a degree in computer science.

Lichelle got a job with a successful computer company. She worked hard and was an asset to the company. It didn't take long for the management to notice her potential. They did not hesitate to give her a transfer and promotion when a vacancy opened in one of their manufacturing outlets.

In her new position, Lichelle could advance as far as she wanted to. Her hard work and dedication were finally beginning to pay off. With higher income, she did what she wanted most: moved Keith out of the old "crime-infested" neighborhood. Although their new suburban neighborhood didn't have a crime problem, it did have another kind of problem—racism.

Lichelle sat on the step and put Keith in her lap. She held his cheeks with both hands to maintain eye contact. "You know, dear, you can talk to me; I'm not only your mother; I'm also your friend."

"Ma, what is wrong with being black?" he asked sobbing. "Why do people hate blacks?" he sniffed. "Why do they treat us badly? What did we do to deserve this?"

Lichelle didn't need to ask Keith what had happened; it was obvious. "Son, do you trust and believe me?" she asked, while wiping the tears off his cheeks. "You know I would never lie to you." Not waiting for a reply, she reassuringly continued, "THERE IS ABSOLUTELY NOTHING WRONG WITH BEING BLACK."

Lichelle slowly rocked Keith trying to put him to sleep. She hoped it would heal, at least temporarily, the hurt of a painful reality. "Why? Why? Why?" she silently asked. Looking at the ceiling, she hoped to miraculously see some answers written on it.

There Is a Crisis

The negative psychological effects of racism on African-Americans have escalated to a crisis. Here are indications of a growing peril:

- The murder rate for African-Americans is alarmingly 48.7%. Teenaged black men and those in their early twenties are "statistically" the highest at risk, according to a Population Reference Bureau report.[1] How can we preserve our race if all the men are dying?

- In 1992, whites murdered 5,967 whites and 392 blacks. Blacks murdered 6,600 blacks and 1,216 whites. These shocking statistics from a *Newsweek* article clearly show that blacks are annihilating each other.[2]

- More than 50% of murder victims in 1993 were black, although African-Americans make up only 12% of the U. S. population.[3]

- Black men are incarcerated at a higher rate in the United States than anywhere else in the world. They have a greater probability of going to prison than to college.[4]

- Almost 50% of black children live in poverty, according to a report by The Children's Defense Fund.[5] Studies indicate that poverty causes poor health, crimes, slow educational development, strained families, teenaged pregnancy, and more. How can we save our little ones from poverty?

- Affirmative action is under attack and may not survive the mounting public opposition. If laws to ensure that minorities are given employment and advancement opportunities are abolished, what is going to prompt companies and organizations to hire or promote blacks?

Prejudice Is Thriving

Many people are quick to believe anything negative about blacks. Two prominent examples reflect people's readiness to assume the worst about African-Americans:

- In November 1994, a young mother from Union, South Carolina, heartlessly murdered her two children. She rolled her car into Lake John D. Long with her children strapped in their protective seats. She alleged that "a black guy" pulled her out of her car at a traffic light and drove off with her children.

- In October 1989, a Boston man gruesomely killed his pregnant wife and shot himself to get insurance money. He told authorities that "a black man" had robbed and shot them. His claim fueled tremendous racial tensions. Police swept through black neighborhoods, interrogated and harassed black men.

What Is Black?

The Merriam-Webster Dictionary gives several definitions for the word "black," among which are: "soiled," "dirty," "wicked," and "evil." Just about everything bad is associated with black: black market, black mail, black eye, black-hole, black-magic, black-death, to name only a few. What is black about illegal transactions? Is deception really black?

The linguistic application of the word "black" has profoundly affected African-Americans. When you connect people with the worst possible characteristic, how do you expect them to act or feel? How do you expect them to be treated? Is it surprising why some blacks go through painful procedures—rhinoplasty (cosmetic nose surgery), bleaching skin, straightening hair, for example—to alleviate the stigma of being black?

The Crisis Affects Us All

Have you ever watched a team win a game? Assuming you have, do you remember what made it victorious? In any game that requires a team, every member's task contributes to the team success or failure. One person alone cannot win a team game; it takes lots of cooperation and communication with other teammates. When a member plays well, he/she makes it easier for others. Everyone can then focus on what he/she does best. Consequently, winning is only a matter of time.

Overcoming racism requires team effort. Civil rights leaders cannot do it by themselves. Every person of color has to contribute—try to be the best that he/she can be. Racism doesn't affect only poor blacks, those in the projects, or those living down South; it affects all blacks. Whether you want to believe it or not, when a brother or sister fails, we all fail.

The Individual's Loss

When people are incarcerated for committing a crime, for example, their productive potentials are adversely affected. Providing for themselves or for their families is almost impossible while in jail.

The Black Population's Loss

Each time one black person does something wrong, racial stereotype is reinforced. Other blacks are stigmatized as if they are responsible. If an African-American disguised as a maintenance man, for example, robbed some tenants in an apartment, you can rest assured that every black maintenance man will be treated with suspicion, even after the offender is behind bars.

As black men continue going to prison, more of the younger generation will start accepting incarceration as the norm. I once overheard a twelve-year-old boy say: "My brother Leo says prison's cool; you get to eat three times a day, plus you work out and watch TV." Paradoxically, young men coming out of prison are regarded as heroes by some of their peers. What do you think will happen when more black children think prison is "cool"?

Successful middle or upper class blacks are also affected when another black fails. Sometimes it may be subtle, but it can hurt all the same. Let's consider an incident with Karen, a black professional in her early twenties. Living in a racially mixed, middle-class suburb, and earning about $50,000 a year, Karen thought that somehow she had risen above racism.

On a January afternoon, Karen and other employees sat watching the 12 o'clock news. In the headlines, nine New Orleans police officers had been arrested for transporting and safe-guarding illegal drugs. Karen secretly hoped they were not black. But her fear was confirmed when they showed the nine officers in handcuffs after the arrest; they were all black. "Why do they have to be black?" Karen thought.

As one officer was led to a waiting car, one of Karen's assistant managers loudly commented: "I knew it; those damn niggers!" Everyone looked at him with shock. When he realized what he had just said, he quickly turned to Karen, who happened to be the only black in the company. "I'm so sorry," he said apologetically. "I didn't know you were sitting there."

The Society's Loss

A person in jail has to be fed, clothed, guarded, provided with medical services and recreational activities. Annually, it costs $22,000 per prisoner in state prisons and $20,000 in federal prisons, according to The National Committee on Community Corrections.[6] Who do you think is paying for this? Taxpayers. Money that could be used on educating people to improve themselves is being spent on incarcerating criminals. A Harvard professor indicated that the United States "spends $7 billion a year to imprison black males, but less than 10 percent of that amount to educate black males."[7]

When some people resort to crime and violence, the society is endangered. People get scared to sleep in their own homes at night; they buy and carry guns around for protection; they get sophisticated alarms and surveillance systems. Even then, they still are not safe. These remedies cannot solve the problem any more than mopping would solve a leaking problem from a broken pipeline.

Recommended Readings

1. Pascoe, Elaine. Racial Prejudice. New York: Franklin Watts, 1985.

2. Mizell, Linda. Think About Racism. New York: Walker, 1992.

Racism cannot destroy people's self-confidence;
but it gives them the opportunity to do so themselves.

THERE IS NOTHING WRONG WITH BEING BLACK

If blacks are as incapable as they are usually portrayed, how do some African-Americans become so successful? There are many blacks—politicians, lawyers, physicians, entertainers, mayors, educators, students, to name a few—who do not reflect the stereotype about black people. Although blacks have to work much harder to succeed, which is due more to social constraints than physical differences, they still manage to become successful.

With the desire and opportunities to succeed, anyone can be successful, regardless of race or national origin. Let's consider some classic examples:

- In the post-Civil War South, Madam C. J. Walker, born in poverty, widowed and a single parent at the age of 19, became the first female African-American millionaire. She was also a philanthropist.[1]

- General Colin Powell rose through a successful military career to become the first African-American Joint Chiefs of Staff chairman. Powell is still popular with both Democrats and Republicans, who continue to offer him political positions and encourage him to run for office.

• Oprah Winfrey's hard work and talent made her very successful in show business. With an estimated worth in excess of $250 million, Oprah is considered the richest woman in the world.[2]

Differences Are Unique

Physical differences are natural. People around the world don't all look alike. Blacks do have some physical characteristics that are different from those of other races or ethnic groups. Asians have physical traits that are different from whites. Eskimos don't resemble Africans. Scandinavians don't look like Hispanics either. And even people within a particular racial or ethnic group look different.

Physical characteristics can, in part, be attributed to evolution from the geographic region of origin. Let's take the body, for example; it maintains temperature. Slender bodies have a tendency to lose more heat than heavier ones. People originating from hot regions—the Sudanese from the Sahara Desert, for example—have tall, thin bodies to dispel heat. People originating from cold regions—the Eskimos, for example—are stocky. Their bodies have to retain heat in freezing temperatures.

The nose is another good example. It adds moisture to the air we breathe. People originating from places with cold, dry air, the Middle East and northern Europe, for example, tend to have longer noses. Why? Because the longer the nose, the more moisture it can add to the air inhaled.[3]

Why do people allow the results of evolution—which once enabled their ancestors to survive—to cause discomfort in their lives today? Physical differences make life more interesting by adding variety. How would you choose a spouse, for example, if everyone looked the same? Could you tell your neighbors apart if they all resembled each other? Physical differences don't necessarily mean good or bad, wrong or right, superior or inferior. Physical differences are essential and should be appreciated and enjoyed, not hated.

Blacks and Capabilities

The Bell Curve, a controversial book written by Charles Murray and the late Richard Herrnstein, claimed that blacks are intellectually inferior. Consequently, blacks are incapable of being economically successful because success depends on "measurable" intelligence. The authors concluded that blacks are destined to poverty because they are not smart enough to get out of it. However, "scholars and testing experts," according to an article distributed by The Associated Press, decided that the authors' facts and statistics are in error.[4]

The authors used scores from Intelligence Quotient (IQ) Tests—exams designed to measure intelligence—to back their allegation that blacks are inferior. IQ tests examined academic literacy rather than the general manner of expression among a group of people.

In the past, blacks found it difficult to get an education. During slavery, educating blacks was illegal. After slavery was outlawed, many blacks were too poor to go to school. Racist groups resisted school integration and often attacked black students and teachers. Is it then baffling why most blacks scored low on a test that examines academic literacy?

Anyway, the test scores were later discovered to be inconsistent—some whites got higher scores than other whites and a socioeconomic factor was considered. Some blacks even outscored some whites. Most whites from the North, whose standards of living were comparably "higher" than their southern counterparts, did better on these tests. Northern blacks got better scores than those from the South. Overall, whites got higher scores than blacks, with the exception of blacks from Kentucky and Ohio, who scored higher than whites from several states. Southern blacks who moved North, over time, showed improvements in their scores.

Statistics are often twisted to back specious claims. Paul R. Ehrlich and S. Shirley Feldman concluded that the comparison results of Black and White IQ scores reflect the "background of the investigator."[5]

Perception and Prejudice

The Random House Dictionary gives the following meaning of perceive: "to become aware of by means of the senses; to understand or form an idea of." "The ability or power to perceive," is one of the definitions the dictionary gives for perception. I, however, think of perception as our interpretation of the people and things around us.

According to *Psychology*, "our past experiences, expectations, and needs," play a role in how we perceive the world around us.[6] If a white lady were mugged in an elevator by a black teenager, for example, she may be afraid to ride another elevator with a black youth.

When people stereotype blacks as thieves, they will be looking for instances to justify their prejudice. If a young black lady were admiring a dress in a department store, for example, the store clerk would probably scrutinize her actions. Her admiration would be interpreted as contemplating shoplifting. Similarly, if a white lady were admiring a dress, the clerk would assume that the lady is interested in buying it. In anticipation of a sale, the clerk would come over to assist.

The Mind Game

Have you ever been ridiculed by your classmates because they didn't like your outfit? Did you hate wearing that outfit afterwards? In my case, my mother bought me pants that my peers thought were "nerdy." So, I always tried to talk her into letting me wear the ones they thought were "cool."

"You act like you don't have any clothes," she would comment. "Why do you want to wear the same clothes over and over?"

I never tried to explain why my friends laughed at my short pants.

When you wear clothes that you feel people don't admire, or ones that you hate, there is a tendency to be self-conscious. If you hear people laughing in a crowd, you get the impression they are making fun of you. You feel depressed until you take off those "horrible" clothes. But, what if the clothes were stuck to your body and you couldn't get them off? How would you feel?

Racism is so successful in affecting blacks because it targets the most conspicuous, the unshedable—the skin. To the racist, black skin color is bad. If you believe that, you'll start to hate yourself because you are black. You feel stuck with an "outfit" that the majority of people hate. Is it a mystery why many blacks are so sensitive? Each time someone makes a racial remark, follows you in a store as if you are a shoplifter, or gets up when you sit next to them, you are reminded that you have an unacceptable skin color. Is it any wonder why the "Black Is Beautiful," positive self-image effort was so successful? Don't let others play with your mind. There is nothing wrong with being black. Black is beautiful!

Recommended Readings

1. Ehrlich, Paul R., and S. Shirley Feldman. <u>The Race Bomb</u>. New York: Quadrangle, 1977.

2. Russel, Kathy, Midge Wilson, and Ronald Hall. <u>The Color Complex</u>. New York: Harcourt, 1992.

We were born to be what we learn to become.

THE REASON PEOPLE ACT IN CERTAIN WAYS

A 17-year-old youth sat trembling in juvenile court awaiting his sentence. The judge knew him well; he was a frequent guest. Unlike other times, he didn't feel quite like the hero his friends thought him to be. In fact, he was scared. He hadn't meant to pull the trigger; the tourist tried to overpower him. "Why didn't that tourist just give me his wallet?" he thought.

About two blocks away from the court, another black youth, not much older than the one above, was packing to go to college. He had received a full scholarship at one of the most prestigious colleges in the country. He graduated valedictorian from his high school. His parents were proud. It was obvious that he would be successful at anything he did.

Both young men in the examples started out as nice, sweet, innocent babies. Notwithstanding, they both have different outlooks on life. Something caused them to do what they did. What influences the choices people make?

Many psychologists and other prominent thinkers—Jean-Jacques Rousseau, for example—believe that heredity is responsible for personality. This view has been twisted to say that some people don't have what it takes. It can be responsible for all the negative stereotypes about blacks. Just because you are black, for example, some people treat you like you are ignorant, although they don't even know you.

Others believe that genetics and environment are both responsible for personality. Anyhow, from observation, environment is obviously the most important determinant of personality. John Locke, a seventeenth-century philosopher, believed that people's minds are like a "blank slate" at birth.[1] People are programmed by their experiences with the world.

People Learn to Be What They Are

I have never met a born gangster. People are not born bad; they learn to become that way. In all my years, I also have never met a racist baby. Babies may be reserved if they don't know you. However, once they get used to you, they don't discriminate by race.

One day, while casually walking through Wal-mart, I noticed two individuals who had captured everyone's attention in the store. One was a little white boy, who couldn't have been more than three years old. He was pulling a black man towards the toy aisles. "Daddy, Daddy," he screamed, "I want the fire truck." The man looked a little uneasy since everyone was staring at them. The kid, on the other hand, didn't seem concerned. He was a bit young to understand the complexity of race relations in society today. I wondered if he would feel self-conscious about his daddy's skin color when he grew up.

If you carefully observe people in society, you will see that they are motivated by other people or things around them. Racism and other forms of discrimination are like everything else; they are learned.

Personality Conforms to Influences

Children are alert and quickly adapt to what they see around them. A mother found her two-year-old daughter with a cigarette in her mouth. Although the cigarette was not lit, the little girl was mimicking her mother smoking.

Many black children are afraid of speaking "correctly" because their peers will tease them about trying to be white. A girl growing up in a music oriented family, Janet Jackson, for example, may also choose a career in entertainment.

Getting out of the projects is difficult, for example, because of all of the adverse factors present. A child growing up in a violent environment, filled with poverty, depression, and drugs, quickly joins right in. The vicious circle can continue through generations if nothing is done to break it.

Why Blacks Were Enslaved

Many social factors contributed to blacks' enslavements. Examining these factors can help us understand the root of blacks' problems. Let's consider the most popular factors. Are you ready for a little history? Here we go:

Acquiring Black Slaves Was Relatively Easy

Like other continents, Africa is inhabited by people of different tribes who speak dissimilar dialects. In Africa, it is common to have several different dialects spoken in an area the size of Rhode Island. The diversity led to frequent tribal wars; prisoners were taken as slaves.

When the Portuguese, Spanish, and other Europeans came to Africa, it was easy to get an unlimited supply of slaves. Many prisoners of war (POWs)—sometimes entire villages or tribes—were captured by other tribes. Because Africans had large families who took care of the daily chores, there wasn't much need for slaves. So, victorious tribes sold their POWs or traded them to the white merchants for tobacco, rum, and smoked fish. Africans also exchanged slaves for guns and ammunition. The new weapons enabled them to efficiently attack other tribes or defend themselves, thereby acquiring more slaves.

There Was an Urgent Need for Manual Labor

The demand for agricultural products—cotton, rice and tobacco—skyrocketed in Europe in the seventeenth century. Plantation owners in the United States needed cheap laborers in order to profit from Europe's demand. Native Americans were unreliable slaves because many of them died from tropical diseases and harsh treatments. Native Americans also were familiar with the area and could easily escape.

Poor European immigrants who worked as indentured servants were not enough; they were not suited for working long hours in the scorching heat, and their work contracts expired after a predetermined number of years—usually seven.

Blacks Were Superior for Plantation Work

Since many Africans grew their own foods, most of them were already familiar with agriculture. Being dark complexioned, blacks could withstand long hours in the sun. Africans were considered physically stronger than Native Americans or poor whites. Africans were foreign to America and had nowhere to run to. Moreover, if blacks did escape, spotting them would be easy.

The Investment Was Profitable

The cost of transporting slaves across the Atlantic was relatively inexpensive. Slaves were crowded in ships' holds. Sanitary conditions were extremely poor. Those who died during the long voyage were thrown overboard.

Buying a slave offered unlimited benefits. Unlike the white indentured servants, blacks became the slave owner's property indefinitely. Blacks were also used for mating; thereby, increasing the owner's slave population.

Blacks could legally be overworked, ill-treated, even killed. Because blacks were not paid for their labor, plantation owners realized huge financial gains.

How Slavery Affected Blacks

Abolishing slavery didn't end black suffering. Many whites favored slavery because their livelihood depended on slave labor. Worst of all, many whites had over the years come to regard blacks as possessions. The thought of seeing blacks free prompted numerous hate crimes. Blacks were terrorized, beaten, and often killed.

Two hundred years of slavery took its toll on black families. Because families were often torn apart and sold, black people may have lost their original family values.

There were other oppressed groups—the Irish immigrants, for example—but blacks were more disadvantaged. Immigrants could get an education. They could get jobs and work their way up. For blacks, the same opportunities were much harder to attain. Blacks found getting an education was difficult and sometimes dangerous. Blacks who integrated white schools were attacked. Racist groups often terrorized black schools.

With no technical skill, limited education, and widespread discrimination, blacks were condemned to the bottom of the social ladder.

The Black Men

Society had always regarded men as heads of households. Black men found it increasingly difficult to live up to their role. During slavery, black men could not protect their wives and children from abuse. Post-slavery wasn't much better either: black men could not provide for their families. Automation had rendered their manual labor obsolete. Industries needed people with technical skills to operate machines. Black men were not prepared for the new challenge. Supporting a family became virtually impossible. Many black men felt useless to their families and deserted them.

A life of crime was the only opportunity for many black men. The world of crime did not discriminate; anyone could try to be a successful criminal. Some black men turned to crime for survival. Others wanted to take out their revenge on society for the mistreatment.

The Black Women

Black women didn't have it easy either. Besides being physically overworked, slave owners often sexually abused them. Their children were torn away to be sold. Their husbands were lynched; they had no one to protect them.

During post-slavery, husbands deserted them. They were left with the children to care for. With little to no support from their husbands, they had to work twice as hard to maintain their families.

The Black Children

With the mother gone all day working, and no father, who gave the children the love and nurture that is so important for their development? Who was there to serve as their role-model?

Many black children grew up confused and frustrated. At home, their families were dysfunctional. In school, people treated them like they were worthless. On the streets, they were treated with suspicion. Pretending to "be tough" eventually became a reality.

Since black children could not prove their masculinity or femininity in school, or in society, they did it the only other possible way—having children. Black children were not prepared for the tremendous responsibility that comes with raising children. How could they care for their young ones when they could barely support themselves? Their children in turn grew up deprived and the whole process repeated itself.

People tend to see themselves in relation to others.

WHY PEOPLE DISCRIMINATE

"Hey buddy! Did you see that guy?" my hyperactive coworker excitedly asked, while hitting my shoulder.

"Hey, easy on my shoulder," I said. "Which guy?" I curiously asked as I backed out of his reach.

"That guy over there; I'm taller than him," Shorty proclaimed.

"So what's the big deal?" I thought. For once, Shorty felt tall. Being merely 5'3", he rarely met another man he could look down on.

Albert Einstein formulated the relativity theory of nuclear energy. Einstein concluded that space and time are not absolute but relative. That physics concept of relativity applies to people also. People are inclined not to see themselves as they really are, but in relation to others. Shorty feels tall when he's around dwarfs, but he feels like a midget when he's around men of average height. You feel financially privileged when you can afford a BMW and your neighbors can't. A racist feels superior only when a "minority" acts inferior.

Large-scale Discrimination

Isolated cases of discrimination are often overlooked, except if they are of great magnitude. However, when discrimination affects a large group of people, it cannot be ignored.

Discrimination breeds hatred and resentment. The consequences of discrimination are unpredictably detrimental; they are a grave threat to national and international peace and stability. The late Dr. Martin Luther King, Jr. once said: "Injustice anywhere is a threat to justice everywhere."

Racism Targets Differences

Many people like to think of discrimination as a black-white problem, but it is not so superficial. If all blacks suddenly turned blue, would racism end? Certainly not. People tend to use any kind of difference as an excuse for discriminating.

If Caucasians were the only race, whites would discriminate against each other on the basis of geographic origin—North and South, for example. Whites within a particular region would discriminate on the basis of hair and/or eye color.

Paradoxically, even African-Americans discriminate against each other. Some light-skinned blacks act as if they are more attractive and intellectually superior to darker-skinned blacks. Black-on-black discrimination is eloquently articulated in Spike Lee's popular film *School Daze.*

Other Discrimination in the United States

Discrimination hasn't been restricted to blacks. Several "non-blacks" also have had their share.

The Catholic Immigrants

The Order of the Star-Spangled Banner, considered by Sharon Elaine Thompson as one of the first organized hate groups in the country, was also called the Know-Nothings—

members were to declare that they knew nothing when questioned about their activities. This hate group targeted Roman Catholic immigrants. They blamed the Catholics for all the socioeconomic changes that accompanied industrialization. As a result:

> Know-Nothings attacked Irish Catholics, stoned their homes, and burned their churches. On election day, armed vigilantes—citizens who organize to punish crime and enforce the law as they see fit—roamed sections of the cities where immigrants lived to prevent the new citizens from voting. [Know-Nothings] feared that once the immigrants became citizens, they would be elected to public office and pass laws that favored the immigrants.[1]

Native Americans

Native Americans suffered discrimination too. The settlers enslaved Native Americans, took their lands and drove them into reservations. Worst of all, the settlers mockingly killed the buffaloes Native Americans depended on for food and clothing.

The Native Americans were unsuccessful in their attempts to resist the mistreatment. Because they consisted of numerous tribes who spoke dissimilar dialects, they were unable to present united resistance.

Wars with the settlers and diseases took their toll on the Native Americans. Many Native Americans were murdered. Three hundred, mostly unarmed Native American women and children were killed, for example, in the battle at Wounded Knee, South Dakota. By the start of the twentieth century, their population had dwindled from one million to a mere three hundred thousand.[2]

The Chinese

The Chinese were the earliest Asian immigrants to arrive in the United States. Their reputation for being industrious and reliable made them preferred laborers. Chinese built the Transcontinental Railroad. However, they were paid only meager wages. People often took advantage of the Chinese because they were foreign, usually spoke little English, had no rights, and were prohibited from testifying in court against whites.

Americans became threatened that the Chinese would take all the jobs; thus began the anti-Chinese movement. Violence against Chinese intensified. Hate groups destroyed Chinese properties, robbed, and even killed many of them. Americans pressured congress into restricting Chinese from coming to the United States. This led to the Chinese Exclusion Act of 1882—a law that banned Chinese immigration for ten years.

Some Chinese who survived all the attacks returned to China. Others moved into segregated neighborhoods called Chinatown, in some American cities.

Discrimination in Other Countries

Prejudice and discrimination are not limited to the United States. People all over the world suffer this painful reality to some extent. While the basis of discrimination—nationality, race, religion, sex, tribe, or color—vary geographically, the processes and consequences of discrimination are strikingly similar.

In India, discrimination is mostly based on caste. People born into a lower caste were stigmatized for life. If they were in a gathering with members of a higher caste, they had to sit separately and sometimes, give up their seats. They also had to sit on lower chairs because they were forbidden to sit "higher" than a member of the upper caste.

The Color of Racism

Members of the lower caste were restricted to specific occupations. Intermarriage between higher and lower caste members was a taboo. Members of the lower caste were not even allowed to touch foods or objects belonging to members of the higher caste; if the contrary occurred, the object was thrown away, or sterilized.[3]

Conditions have tremendously improved for lower caste members in India today. The people are more tolerant of each other. Members of the lower caste now have privileges that were once reserved only for members of the upper caste. Moreover, the government recognizes the importance of education in alleviating social oppression and is actively assisting lower caste members with schooling.

However, some members of the higher caste have exhausted, to little avail, just about every possible means to keep the old system intact.

In Bosnia, the Croats and Serbs continue to violently attack and murder each other. The country is torn apart by the civil conflicts. Everyone is at risk. The catastrophic result of animosity escalates because the Roman Catholic Croats, the Sunni Muslim and Eastern Orthodox Serbs allowed their religions and national origins to tragically impair a peaceful coexistence.

In the Middle East, the Jews and Arabs—originating from the same geographic area—have a history of conflict dating back to biblical times. Prior to the early twentieth century, Jews were scattered around the world in diaspora. They were targets for discrimination and hate crimes. The Nazis murdered over six million Jews in the Holocaust of World War II.

When Jews finally started returning to their homeland in Palestine—a movement called Zionism—the Arabs living there began to protest. The new arrivals and Arabs peacefully coexisted at first, but as the number of Jews increased, so did hatred and discrimination. The Arabs feared the increasing presence of Jews would interrupt their way of life.

Arabs and Jews allowed religion and nationality to ignite several wars, raids, and terrorist attacks. Many innocent lives—both Arabs and Jews—were extinguished as a result. Arabs and Jews are presently negotiating for peace. But, some groups—the Hamas, a Palestinian Islamic organization, for example—have committed numerous terrorist attacks against Israel to oppose the peace talks.

Liberia, a country once recognized for its stability within the African continent, is now in ruins after a gruesome civil war that erupted around 1990. About two-thirds of the population are now believed to be refugees.

The root of the conflict can be traced back to the Americo-Liberians—a mostly light-skinned group of people who originated from freed American slaves. Americo-Liberians discriminated against the indigenous people. Intermarriage between the two groups was frowned upon for several years. Opportunities were basically reserved for Americo-Liberians.

Up until 1980, when the Americo-Liberian regime was finally terminated by a bloody coup, the government had been run solely by them. Americo-Liberians claimed to have had democratic leadership, but, it was more like oligarchy.

The indigenous government that took over soon started the same discrimination practices that Americo-Liberians were notorious for. Only this time, discrimination was based on tribal origin. People quickly became intolerant. The government, consisting mostly of members of the Khran tribe, was threatened and did not want to give up control. Other tribal groups were not willing to be continually dominated. Mounting hatred escalated beyond control; massacre became the order of the day.

Fear and Discrimination

Fear, "an unpleasant often strong emotion caused by expectation of danger," as defined by *The Merriam-Webster Dictionary*, is a basic and universal emotion. Many occurrences and situations can cause fear, but people's reaction to fear is what *Psychology* terms the fight-or-flight reaction.[4]

When people are faced with what they perceive as "threatening," they may take an active role—fight. In the case of racism, fear can involve, but is not limited to, hiding under a white hood and bedsheet, burning crosses, and attacking, sometimes even killing, others who are considered a threat.

Comparably, the reaction to fear can be passive—flight. Again with respect to racism, it is trying to separate from others who are perceived as threatening. This separatism was prevalent during the times of Jim Crow laws. Blacks had to live in specific neighborhoods and use separate facilities. Blacks and whites were even buried in different cemeteries.

Today, flight has taken on an unusual form: large number of people leaving the cities for the more expensive suburbs; real estate brokers collectively agreeing not to sell houses in some neighborhoods to blacks; raising the qualifying standards to exclude most blacks from financing homes in some areas, and more.

Fear of Freedom

Southern whites feared freeing blacks because of all the inevitable changes that would follow. As we all know, changes can be scary because people tend to cling to the familiar. Here are some reasons that fueled that fear:

Possibility of Revenge

During the days of slavery, blacks were ruled harshly. Blacks were humiliated, sold, cursed, sexually abused, and often lynched. Many whites feared free blacks would avenge the injustice.

Loss of Power

The agricultural southern economy relied on slave labor. White families acquired considerable wealth because maintaining slaves was relatively low compared with the revenues generated from slave labors. For most southern whites, abolishing slavery meant losing control over their financial assets.

Economic Change

The depressed economy would limit the number of available jobs. If blacks were allowed to compete for these openings, whites would have fewer jobs.

Social Change

If blacks were allowed to live as whites, they would soon flood white neighborhoods. If intermarriage were permitted, eligible white bachelors would have to compete with blacks for those pretty single white women.

Justifying Hate

If you have ever been through a divorce or know someone who has been, you will be able to relate to the resentment that arises between spouses during this critical time. In an attempt to terminate a marriage, a husband and/or wife often comes up with hideous allegations to discredit his/her spouse.

Likewise, when it comes to racism, people can be at their worst. The dominant group comes up with all kinds of accusations to justify hating other groups. In the United States, for example, some whites argued that blacks were too stupid to educate, so why bother? After the depression in Europe, Hitler was able to convince a large segment of the population that the Jews were the cause of Germany's economic problems. He had a solution which met little resistance.

The Ultimate Result of Discrimination

Discrimination breeds hatred. Hatred blossoms into a desire to annihilate anyone who is perceived as a threat. To stay alive, the instinct for survival causes oppressed people to retaliate. Destruction can be enormously unpredictable. Law and order cannot dominate when people are destroying each other. As a result, chaos takes control.

Discrimination and You

People will always discriminate, judge you, and evaluate you. If they do so fairly, based on your behavior and values, you can accept their evaluation. If they do so unfairly, because of prejudice or racism, then you are best off ignoring their evaluation. Don't let discrimination deteriorate your self-value.

Seeing may be believing,
but consistently seeing and hearing are convincing.

THE MEDIA AND MASS DISCRIMINATION

The media—"means of communication, as radio and television, newspapers, magazines, [internet, and other sources of information], that reach or influence very large number of people," as defined by *The Random House Dictionary*—contributes tremendously to people's attitude about racism within the society. Virtually everyone is bombarded by the media's influences. How many families do you know who do not watch television? If you know any, how many of them do not listen to the radio, read newspapers or magazines?

African-Americans and other minorities are stigmatized when the media exaggerates degrading news about them. In order to successfully guard against the media's derogatory influences, you have to understand how the media operates.

The Media

The media prospers by providing information to the public. Reporters, journalists, editors, writers and camera crews, for example, are often professionals whose objective is to make a living keeping the public informed. They don't purposely attempt to humiliate, degrade, or use anyone—with the exception of talk shows, talk radio, and the almighty tabloids. The media, like every other organization, has expenses. They have fixed overhead: rent or mortgage, utilities, salaries, to name a few. Without revenues they cannot survive. The big question is: how does the media get money? For newspapers and magazines, their returns come from selling their product(s). The more readership they have, the more money they make. They can also generate substantial revenues from advertising.

For the radio and television, their popularity comes from ratings. Ratings depend basically on the size of the audience; the larger the audience, the higher the ratings. Ratings are also used to determine advertising rates because businesses want to use popular programs which will give their product(s) and/or service(s) maximum publicity.

In recent years, we have seen a surge of keen competition within the information industry. ABC, CBS, and NBC are no longer the sole television giants, for example. There are literally hundreds of cable networks competing. The competition is also noticeable in the magazine and newspaper market. You can probably remember when *Ebony* and *Jet* were the most popular black magazines. Today, there is *Essence, Emerge, Black Enterprise*, and many other African-American magazines.

What does all the competition mean? Good for the consumers because they have more options. Television fanatics like me can flip through channels. Comparably, the competition is challenging for the media; they have to strive harder to attract audiences.

How the Media Attracts Audiences Amidst Stiff Competition

How does the media attract audiences amidst stiff competition? By giving the audiences what they want, the media becomes competitive. If the audiences want racism, violence, sex, you name it, the media gives it to them. Why? When the media satisfies audiences' needs—tells them what they want to hear, shows them what they want to see—the media has a better chance of capturing loyalty; thereby, increasing sales and/or ratings.

Since the media's financial goal depends on captivating the largest audiences, whose patronage will they concentrate on? The "majority" or the mostly poor "minorities"? By exploiting minorities' shortcomings—poverty, violence, drugs, to name only a few—the media attracts a larger majority audience. News of minorities' successes or accomplishments are rarely publicized. However, when such news is presented, it usually occupies a small column in the back pages or a minute segment of airtime. Whereas, news of minorities' failures or problems seems constantly to make front page or lead stories.

The media preys on the fact that people generally tend to enjoy seeing the faults in others; it diverts their attention from their own imperfections. Have you noticed how news about someone's downfall seems to attract much publicity—the O. J. Simpson murder trial, for example. A constant reminder of someone else's misfortune enables many people to feel fortunate.

Although the media increases audiences by focussing on, and to some extent exaggerating blacks' problems, the trade-offs reinforce racism.

The Media Is Often "Bad News" for Blacks

The consistent derogatory stereotypes about blacks, especially those exaggerated out of proportion by the media, are implanted in audiences' minds. Consequently, the devastating effects of racism are aggravated.

How the Media Influence People's Perceptions of African-Americans

Each time whites or people of non-black origin encounter the media portrayal of negative African-American images, stereotypes about blacks are reinforced. People's perceptions of African-Americans have a tremendous impact on discrimination. During slavery, the slave masters' perceptions of a particular slave determined whether that slave would be privileged to be assigned house duties, condemned to the fields, or sold.

Today, people's perceptions of you determine, to a large extent, whether they will elect you as governor, promote you to a supervisory position, call you the "N" word, or treat you like a criminal. Because people act in accordance with their beliefs, a convincing negative portrayal of African-Americans stimulates discriminatory reactions.

A white owner of an apartment complex, for example, who wants to change all the locks, may give the contract to a white locksmith. Is he/she racist? The owner may be scared that a black locksmith will retain a master key to rob the tenants. Somewhere in his/her mind the idea that "blacks are criminals" may lurk. But are there no white criminals? There are dishonest people in every race, but the emphasis, according to the media, is not white crooks but blacks. And people remember what the media consistently shows and tells them.

An honest African-American locksmith, on the other hand, may rarely get a contract. He/she can end up feeling inadequate because of not being able to make ends meet. Is it a "big secret" why some African-Americans are too frustrated to even try?

The Media Bias Influences African-Americans' Perceptions of Themselves

The consistent media portrayal of negative African-American images derogates blacks' self-value. "The practices of media distortion may affect the self-esteem of young African-Americans in negative ways," according to Dr. Camille Cosby in *Television's Imageable Influences*.[1] The repetitive biased presentation of African-Americans by the media is programmed into some blacks' minds. Consequently, some African-Americans involuntarily conform to the media's definition of blacks like they would respond to a hypnotist.

Any repetitive suggestion, especially a convincing one, is apt to become a reality. If you have always been told and treated like you are stupid, you will most likely believe that you are dull and act accordingly. "Negative ideas have exactly the same effect upon our behavior as the negative ideas implanted into the mind of a hypnotized subject by a professional hypnotist," according to the late Dr. Maxwell Maltz, in *Psycho-Cybernetics*. Dr. Maltz gave the following description of negative programming:

> The hypnotist tells a football player that his hand is stuck to the table and that he cannot lift it. It is not a question of the football player "not trying." He simply cannot. He strains and struggles until the muscles of his arm and shoulder stand out like cords. But his hand remains fully rooted to the table.

[The hypnotist] tells the champion weight-lifter that he cannot lift a pencil from the desk. And although normally [the weight-lifter] can hoist a 400 pound weight overhead, he now actually cannot lift the pencil. Strangely enough, in the above instances, hypnosis does not weaken the athletes. They are potentially as strong as ever. But without realizing it consciously they are working against themselves. On one hand they "try" to lift their hand, or the pencil, by voluntary effort, and actually contact the proper lifting muscles. But on the other hand, the idea "you cannot do it" causes contrary muscles to contract quite apart from their will. The negative idea causes them to defeat themselves—they cannot express, or bring into play their actual available strength.[2]

Some African-Americans' response to biased media influences is voluntary. Some blacks may decide to act like gangsters. "Hey, people already treat us like gang members," they may say, "we might as well be."

Countering Media-Biased Influences

Can the media's negative bias about African-Americans be alleviated? Well, some people believe that an increased presence of African-Americans in the media—journalists, anchor persons, camera crews, editors—will help alleviate the bias in the media. Around the late 60's, the National Advisory Commission on Civil Disorders—a committee also called the Kerner Commission, appointed by President Lyndon Johnson to investigate the causes of racial unrest—mandated the media to hire African-Americans in a proportional number to the black population. The media eventually hired more African-Americans.

Today, some African-Americans have highly visible roles in the media—Bryant Gumbel hosts the *Today* show, Ed Bradley on *60 Minutes*, Oprah Winfrey in her talk show, Bill Cosby and the popular *Cosby Show*, to name only a few. But did the commission's recommendation improve racism in the media?

The "media portrayal of African-Americans are no better today than they were [in the past]," according to Kenneth Walker, an independent television producer and columnist. "On most news programs, African-Americans are still described as far more violent, less industrious and less religious than we actually are." Kenneth continues, "We are still largely portrayed as drug dealers, gang members and welfare queens."

Kenneth Walker, who is also a veteran national news broadcaster, believes that racism is abundant within the media. African-American broadcast journalists, for example, are discouraged from making suggestions. "Often the sole `rewards' we receive for trying to point our white colleagues in the direction of a strong story are reputations as being `pains in the butt,' `troublemakers' or `difficult to work with' or having `an attitude problem'."[3]

So what is the solution to eliminating the bias in the media?

You Are the Solution

You have more control over the bias in the media than you know. You can positively influence the media's negative portrayal of African-Americans. Here's how you can take control of the real definition of African-Americans:

- Decide to be successful and overcome racism. Live up to your definition of yourself. As long as you are being who you want to be, you cannot be who the media wants you to be. The media cannot destroy your reputation without tarnishing evidence against you, or the media will be opening up to a libel lawsuit.

- Be aware that the media is out hunting for news, especially degrading, negative and controversial news. Don't give the media the opportunity to profit at your downfall. Consider possible consequences before you act. The little argument with your buddy doesn't have to end in a gunfight.

- All that you see on the television, all that you read in the newspapers, books and magazines, and all that you hear on the radio, are not necessarily the almighty truth. The media is operated by people; hence, there is the propensity for personal prejudice. Be critical of information you receive from the media. Always use your better judgment before accepting news as facts.

- Voice your concern to the media. Don't just let the media portray you any way they want. Write to the editors, networks, or stations and complain about their biased representation of African-Americans. Let the media know that you deserve a fair coverage. As a consumer, you have a right to request an unbiased presentation of African-Americans.

- Don't patronize racism in the media. If a particular show degrades you or the general African-American image, don't watch it. If a radio station demeans African-Americans, tune to another station. If a newspaper is obsessed with derogating African-Americans' image, don't read it. Dr. Camille Cosby, for example, canceled her subscription to a daily newspaper in New York because of the paper's derogatory depiction of African-Americans.[4]

If those most affected do not remedy the problem,
those least affected are less likely to do so.

OVERCOMING RACISM

Before successfully undertaking any problem, preparation is essential, even more so when the problem is as complex as racism.

Let's investigate some areas that will help you prepare to tackle racism from the core:

Stop the Blaming

As far back as the incident in the Garden of Eden—assuming you are familiar with the story—people have been blaming each other. Eve blamed the serpent for tempting her to eat the forbidden fruit, and Adam blamed Eve for tempting him. People have a tendency to blame others.

Blaming is counterproductive. When you blame people, you attribute the faults to them, hence, the solution. Unfortunately, people rarely want to take blame; they are quick to shift it onto someone else.

Overcoming your own prejudice enables you to overcome prejudice in others. OK, blacks were once enslaved by whites. But how are whites today responsible for what their ancestors did to yours years ago? Blaming the new white generation is

---

much like someone blaming all blacks for what another black did. You don't want to be prejudged, so you should avoid labeling all whites as racists. Indeed, some whites are racists, but some blacks are racists too.

All the blaming in the world will not solve African-American crime, drug or unemployment problems. Blaming cannot give you equality; neither will it make people like you. Blaming doesn't even make you happy; rather, it only promotes resentment. While you are busy pointing a finger at everyone else, who is solving the problem?

The damage is done; dwelling on racism doesn't help anyone. Instead, you should strive to overcome racism by utilizing your time for constructive purposes.

Redefining Black

Some blacks frequently accuse other blacks of trying to be white when they are not being *black*. Just because you are black doesn't mean that you have to walk a certain way, pull on your crotch, listen to rap music only, or speak in slang. You cannot overcome racial stereotype by stereotyping yourself.

You are a creative and complex individual. You should not feel compelled to conform to only one mode of behavior. Creativity in any endeavor is not a "white" thing; it is personal and also universal. Exploring and developing your potential in whatever calling you choose is a birthright.

The greatest hindrances to advancements are not the barriers that others erect for you, but the mental obstacles that you put up for yourself. Franklin D. Roosevelt had a similar opinion on destiny: "Men [and women] are not prisoners of fate, but only prisoners of their own minds." If you believe that blacks are good only in sports, for example, you may tirelessly train and practice until you achieve excellence in the desired sport activity. Whereas, you may perform poorly in "non-sport" activities because of not applying yourself.

You must not limit yourself; if some African-Americans can excel in sports, you can do the same. You can dominate any occupation by devoting the diligence some African-Americans apply to sports.

You should define "black" in terms of capabilities and possibilities rather than restricting yourself to stereotypes. You must encourage fellow African-Americans to advance in new activities. Do not tease them for breaking away from the stereotype. By overpowering your own stereotype, you can alleviate the effects of racism. Respect individualism, not stereotypes.

Equality Starts from within

Many African-Americans often complain about equality. In their yearning for equality, they look to congress, civil rights leaders, and politicians. Instead, they get disappointments. Why? Because anti-discrimination laws, politics, or affirmative action programs cannot bestow equality. However, legal measures give African-Americans opportunities to earn equality.

Laws can oblige businesses to hire and promote you, but that doesn't solve the equality problem. Working next to a white person or supervising one doesn't necessarily give you a sense of equality. If you feel inferior, you will act inferior, thereby, reinforcing racism.

You cannot gain equality when you are struggling to survive on minimum wage. You do not feel equal when other blacks are butchering each other. You feel less than equal when stray bullets pierce the life out of your children as they play.

The big question is: how do you gain equality? Equality starts from within. You alleviate impartiality when you advance yourself professionally, become competitive, expand your capabilities, encourage others to succeed, and become the best you can be. When others see your personal and professional advancements, they will almost automatically give you the respect and equality that you deserve.

Strive to Be a Positive Role Model

Whether you believe that you are a role model or not, you really are. People around you, especially the children, are watching you. If you act inferior, they will notice. People who look up to you may adopt your inferior attitude. Some people will take advantage of your inferiority complex by demeaning you. Others may despise you because of your attitude.

Strive to set a positive example. Every situation offers you an opportunity to prove that you can be a commendable role model. When you demonstrate mastery over racism, others will be encouraged to follow suit. As you succeed, you will be moving closer to overcoming racism.

Love Yourself

"Them white folks don't like blacks," some African-Americans often proclaim. So what? Will white people's love for you pay your bills? In fact, some whites don't even like other whites—"poor white trash," for example. Some people hate Jews, some blacks despise Vietnamese, some Chinese hate Japanese, some blacks even dislike other blacks.

Loving and accepting yourself is more important than someone else's love and acceptance for you. Whites' hatred for blacks doesn't inject drugs into your veins. You destroy yourself when you feel worthless and hate yourself.

You have to love and respect yourself. You should get involved in practices that enhance your mind and body, not those that only destroy you. Sports, reading, dancing, and other physical and mental activities help you build self-esteem.

Don't worry about someone not loving you. When you love yourself, you will constantly seek personal improvement. Moreover, you will become happy with yourself. Only then will you make other people happy. And when you make people happy, they will love and admire you. So, concentrate on loving yourself first. You can overcome the self-hatred racism causes by self-love.

Support Each Other

A large number of businesses in black neighborhoods are owned and operated by non-blacks—Vietnamese, Chinese, Italians, for example. Blacks are just as capable of being successful entrepreneurs.

So why do many black businesses fail? Entrepreneurs, especially blacks, need patronage to sustain their businesses. Black entrepreneurs generally receive little support from society. Moreover, some blacks would rather patronize a "non-black" business because they feel that black products and/or services are not good enough—the negative effect of racism.

There is money to be made in black communities or non-black merchants wouldn't be there. African-American businesses can prosper and at the same time provide employment opportunities for other blacks. But you must encourage fellow African-Americans to reach for financial freedom by patronizing them financially, spiritually and emotionally. Others just may do the same for you.

Can you imagine what will happen when more African-Americans succeed in their own businesses? The action will snowball. Blacks will have greater control over their economic

Overcoming Racism

status. African-American unemployment will be alleviated. More African-Americans will be motivated to succeed.

When you take control of your economic successes, racism will not be able to take control of you. By supporting fellow African-Americans, you counter the disunity racism causes.

Switch the Mindset

"I am black; therefore, I must succeed," should be your attitude, rather than, "I cannot succeed because I'm black." When you decide to go after success, you take control of your destiny. Your mindset and efforts go into accomplishing results. Whereas, if you feel that your skin color is barring you from succeeding, your conviction becomes self-fulfilling.

You must make a commitment to excellence in everything that you do. Racism cannot make you feel worthless when you prove to yourself that you are a valuable citizen. Controlling your successes enables you to control racism.

Control the Hurt

African-Americans have experienced so much hurt. And that hurt will only escalate if we do not utilize every available opportunity to advance ourselves.

When you hurt inside, you tend to pass your negative feelings onto other people. This only alienates you by making people miserable around you. Uncontrolled hurt can lead to physical aggression. Violence, however, is not the solution. When you attack someone, he/she will often fight back.

You have to be tactful when you are hurting. You must control hurtful feelings by redirecting them to accomplish positive results—overcoming racism.

You shape your life with decisions which are based on
one of two little words: "yes" and "no."

GOOD DECISIONS TURN DREAMS INTO REALITIES

Little Hanna Mae loves to go shopping. Whenever she becomes captivated by a toy, she says: "aaaiiih, Dadda, I want." Upon my approval, she picks up the toy—if it isn't bigger than she—and holds onto it tight. She refuses to let anyone help her. Hanna Mae keeps collecting toys until her little arms are full. But she doesn't stop there. She often drops some toys to make room for more. Hanna's mom and I often debate on which toys she will end up with. Hanna Mae usually drops everything when she gets fatigued from toting an armful around the store.

When it comes to decision making, some people don't quite grow out of their childhood behavior. They make decisions on impulse. They want everything. They go after every desire which fascinates them, only to ultimately relinquish their efforts.

Other people go through life with the notion: *Ala bab Allah*—Arabic for "What will be, will be; leave it to God." And they expect God to come down and make their decisions. But from biblical history, God intended for you to make your own decisions. That's why you have the ability to choose between "right" and "wrong."

With only one life to live, you don't have enough time to go after every desire. You should focus only on decisions that are important for your development, happiness and well-being. Moreover, when you are going after every desire, you can easily lose sight of your priorities.

In order for you to achieve success in overcoming racism, you have to make accurate, timely, and beneficial decisions. Because if you don't do so, you are doomed to the mercy of those who do.

Using the Two Simple Words

Every decision—simple or complex—that you make boils down to either a "yes" or "no." However, arriving at that "yes" or "no" isn't always as simple as the words themselves. Some decisions are rewarding, some decisions impose on you tremendously, and some decisions are painful. Being successful at overcoming racism requires skill; you have to know when to say "yes" and when to say "no."

Considering your wants and needs will simplify the decision making process. Start by asking yourself if the possible outcome of your decision contributes towards obtaining your goal. If it does, make the right decision. If it doesn't, don't make the wrong decision.

Consider the Consequences Before Making Decisions

Would you jump into a swimming pool without first feeling how cold the water is? Well, at times, some of us do. Making a decision without knowing what you are getting into is ludicrous, and sometimes dangerous.

Before you commit to a "yes" or "no," try to consider possible consequences. This deliberation could completely change your decision. Let's use the drunk driving scenario, for example. If you consider only the thrill and stupor you are dying to feel, you probably wouldn't hesitate to drive drunk. Whereas, if you stop to consider the possibility of abruptly disrupting innocent lives, getting arrested, going to jail, losing your driving privileges, and living with guilt for the rest of your life, you would change your mind about driving while under the influence.

Your decisions and subsequent actions can either help alleviate or reinforce racism. Moreover, due to stereotypes, other blacks are also affected—positively or adversely—by decisions you make. You should consider the possibility of causing irreparable damage when you make decisions. Don't treat decisions lightly. If your decisions counter the effects of racism, you will soon realize the victory of overcoming racism.

Differentiate Your Needs and Wants

You may want a Lexus, some fancy clothes, lots of money, a house in the Virgin Islands, and the list can go on without end. But what do you need? Your wants can have a major impact on your ability to achieve your dreams.

If you are not careful, your wants can immobilize you. Wants can tempt you to go so far into debt, for example, that you barely have enough money left to buy necessities. Consequently, you get all tensed up when the bills start arriving.

Since people generally want more than they need or could possibly afford, you should concentrate on your needs. As you ascend the success ladder, you will be in a better position to afford your wants. If you need transportation only to get to work, for example, diving into debt for a brand new Cadillac is not practical. If you need only to satisfy your hunger, eating at the most expensive restaurant every day is not logical.

Differentiating your wants and needs helps you focus on priorities. You must guard against becoming enslaved by your wants. You cannot overcome racism when you are financially or socially stagnant. First, focus on your needs and the rest will follow.

Don't Follow a Bad Decision Through

Two negatives equal a positive only in algebra. In real life, you cannot rectify a wrong decision by making another wrong one. Sometimes when some people discover that they have made a mistake, they aggravate the situation by making more mistakes.

The first rule of righting a wrong decision is: STOP! "If you find yourself in a hole, stop digging." Analyze the damage. Investigate your possibilities. Take immediate action(s) to correct the mistake(s).

Never hesitate to change your course of action, if the present one is obviously taking you to a "dead end." Your actions will not take care of themselves; you have to take care of them. Overcoming racism requires making worthwhile decisions and correcting "wrong" ones.

Embrace Change

People can become so complacent in their "comfort zone" that they are afraid to try anything new, even if it's in their best interest. Times are rapidly changing; technologies are advancing exponentially. The ways by which you accomplish your wants or needs are also being affected. Unless you adapt to the changing society, your progress will be frozen; hence, you will not be able to overcome racism.

You have to break away from the enslavement of the old system to grab onto the new one. If you are on welfare and having more babies just to exploit the system, for example, you are only entrapping yourself and hurting your children. Moreover, you are increasing racial stereotypes; taxpayers don't appreciate their hard-earned money being abused. You can take advantage of one or several federal programs and aids to become more self-reliant.

Strive to become efficient in your daily activities by using every available means. If the old ways aren't getting you the desired results, it's time to try a new approach.

Base Your Decisions on Facts

Gambling is thrilling, but it can also be very costly. Basing your decisions on "scanty" information is much like gambling. You cannot afford to be a loser because that reinforces racial stereotype. You can decrease the odds of overcoming racism by basing all of your decisions and actions on facts.

The information superhighway—internet, for example—has made acquiring facts easier than ever. There is no need to blindly make decisions when you have pertinent information at your fingertips.

Whether you want to buy a vacation, get health insurance, get financial aid for college, or move into a new neighborhood, do your homework; get the facts. What you don't know could cost you dearly. There is no excuse for not knowing the facts. Make it your business to know as much as possible about what you want. Only then can you take full advantage of opportunities.

Consider how easy making the right decision is, compared with correcting a wrong decision. You should make every effort to investigate your options before jumping to a decision.

Make Your Own Decision

"Should I marry her?" "Should I buy these slacks?" "Should I take the job?" These are only some of the questions people ask others when they are faced with making a decision. How does your buddy know exactly what you want in a potential partner? Why should Mom make your decision on marriage, when you will be living with your spouse? Why should your girlfriend decide which dress you should wear?

Some people want others to make decisions for them. This is a problem. Since people usually base their decisions on their own perceptions and expectations, their decisions may not be in your best interest.

Allowing people to make your decision is quite different from getting an opinion. The latter is advisable because other people's opinions enable you to see possibilities from their perspectives.

One of the goals of racism is to make African-Americans feel incapable. You will definitely feel incompetent when other people are making the decisions that shape your life. Making your own decisions gives you more control over your life; therefore, you overcome racism.

You have opportunities to make your own decisions. Since you are usually the one who bears the consequences of your decisions, be the one to make your decisions. Don't be afraid to make decisions. You may make some bad decisions, but don't we all? As with everything else, your judgment and confidence will improve with practice and time. You can decide to take control of your life and overcome racism; please, don't throw that away.

Don't Act on Impulse

Sometimes you have years to make a decision; other times, you may have days, several hours, or minutes. But, at times, all you will have is a split second—avoiding a wreck, for example. In such instances, you don't have time to think, you just act. And your action has to be appropriate for the prevailing circumstances.

Every decision requires some degree of planning. In most cases, you will have enough time to make a decision. At all cost, avoid making decisions on impulse unless you are obligated to do so. You are most likely to make better decisions when you are prepared than when you are not.

Organizations where success depends on employees making decisions on impulse—rescue services, airlines, the military, to name a few—recognize the importance of preparation in making decisions in an emergency. Such organizations use extensive simulation training to prepare their employees to make quick and accurate decisions. The simulated scenario enables the employees to practice making impulse decisions in a non-threatening situation. The employees are prepared to make decisions when a real emergency pops up.

If you have time to investigate your options, do not decide on impulse. Sleep on a decision if you have to. If the salesman is persuading you to buy a car that you have doubts about, ask for his business card and tell him you want to think things over. If you want to beat up your boss for using racial slurs, consider the possible consequences of your action.

Don't allow yourself to get pressured into doing anything you don't quite feel comfortable with. Getting away from a tempting situation enables you to be more logical. Racists proclaim that: "Blacks act on impulse; they cannot think." By not giving in to impulse, you gain greater control over your decisions; hence, you overcome racial stereotypes.

Don't Get Emotional

Emotions will cloud your reality if you let them. When you are faced with a decision, emotions will influence you unless you guard against them. A black man ended up buying a house more expensive than he could comfortably afford, for example, not because he liked the house, but because the real estate agent treated him like a "poor black." To prove otherwise, the man signed the papers.

Racists will try to control you by manipulating your emotions—trying to make you feel worthless. Don't get emotional because you will lose control over your better judgment. Knocking someone out for calling you a "nigger" is not worth getting arrested for, or going to jail for. Control your emotions by being rational. Know what you want and don't let emotions or racism steal that away from you. Reacting in a positive manner to any negative situation yields superior results.

Success is in the attitude, not in the skin color.

YOU CAN GET WHAT YOU REALLY WANT

Many people tend to get irrational when they cannot get what they want. Whether you want equality, companionship, respect, love, fame and fortune, you name it, allowing yourself to become erratic doesn't help you achieve your dreams. Whereas, if you follow your heart with the "right" attitude, you'll discover how easy being successful really is. This chapter and subsequent ones will show you how to effectively develop the "success" attitude.

Success Is Colorless

Some African-Americans complain of not being able to succeed in life because they are the "wrong" color. That is precisely what racists want them to believe. But look around you. Although a disproportionate number of blacks are poor, many African-Americans are financially well-off. Successful people come in all colors.

Accomplishment Is a Process

A process is a combination of actions that leads to a specific result. Accomplishing anything, including overcoming racism, involves a process. You cannot wave a magic wand and "poof" racism is instantly abolished from your life. You have to first believe that you are capable of success before you can overcome racism. As your actions yield desired results, your belief in your capabilities will strengthen.

The key to making any process work for you is to break it into smaller parts. Focusing on the individual parts makes them manageable. If you wanted to recover from a drug problem, for example, you would concentrate on getting help first. Then focus on breaking away from your circle of influence. Next, you try to become reliable, get a job, and so forth. If the individual parts are done right, the result will follow suit.

Try out Possibilities

There are as many solutions, if not more, than there are wants. While some wants have only one solution, others have several. African-Americans' only solution to realizing true equality and happiness is to overcome racism. However, there are numerous solutions to overcome racism: unity, self-respect, education, determination, to name only a few.

A lady I'll call Aretha experienced an unexpected financial setback. She and her children would be evicted in two days if she didn't come up with last month's rent. Her options were: borrow the rent money from cousin Patrice, get an advance from her work, or apply for a loan from the local bank or finance company.

Anyway, cousin Patrice was broke and couldn't help, but she did offer Aretha and the children a place to stay. The finance company rejected Aretha's application because she didn't have a credit history. Her boss told her that salary advance was against company policy. Aretha was disappointed. She felt reluctant to try the bank because its qualification standard was more stringent than finance companies. Aretha decided to give the bank a try anyway. Fortunately, the bank was engaged in a massive marketing campaign, and had considerably lowered loan qualification standards. Aretha got her loan and was happy; she hated to have to impose on cousin Patrice.

Don't be reluctant to try out possibilities. Do not underestimate or take any possibility for granted, unless you have substantial evidence to do so. Interestingly, the possibility that you least expect to work out just may. Just because you don't have a checking account doesn't mean that some local bank or finance company will not approve your loan application. Just because your relatives are poor doesn't mean that several of them cannot come up with enough money to loan you. Just because you are black doesn't mean that you always have to work hard for so little.

If one possibility doesn't work out, don't get discouraged. You haven't failed; the possibility simply didn't work out. You can always try another option. You fail only if you give up trying. Use every failure as an opportunity to learn. Find out why you were unsuccessful. The lessons you learn from failures can make your next venture a success.

When considering possibilities, always remember, the worst that could happen is that you do not get what you want. The best that could happen, you achieve your goal. Ask yourself if trying out a possibility will help you overcome racism. If an option can help you, don't hesitate to try it out. If an option cannot help you, don't waste your time; find another that will help.

Failure Is the Foundation for Success

Show me a successful person and I will show you a person who learned from failures. Spike Lee's first project *Messenger* was a failure. Lee had completed the script, hired actors, actresses, and even a camera crew, but it all fell through because he could not come up with enough money to finance his project. He learned from the failure of *Messenger*. His next project was a big success. Using a simpler approach that required fewer characters and less expenses, *She Gotta Have It* made more than $7 million.[1]

Racism will defeat African-Americans only when blacks feel and act like failures. But failure is not an automatic condemnation; it means only that you have to try a different approach. If you are working three or more jobs and still not getting anywhere, then maybe the solution is acquiring a lucrative skill and/or getting a promotion.

When someone asked Thomas Edison—considered "the most prolific inventor" because he invented the duplicating process, electric power plant, electron tubes, microphones, motion pictures, the electric light, storage battery, and more— why he continued to try making a new battery after repeated failures, he answered: "Failures, I have no failures. Now I know 50,000 ways it won't work!"

Sometimes, you will get what you want the first time you try; sometimes you will have to try more than once. Whereas, if you don't try at all, you don't stand a chance of accomplishing anything worthwhile. You are not a failure; don't let racism make you feel like a failure. You are capable of success.

Be Willing to Pay the Price

There is a price tag attached to everything you get in life. Some people say: "Nothing in America is free," or "There is no such thing as a free lunch." You have to pay either directly or indirectly, with money, service, or time for everything you want. If you order a pizza, you pay the price with money. You get a promotion because you have paid the price by working hard in your position. When you commit a crime, you pay the price by doing the time.

Overcoming racism has a price tag too. You have to persevere. You have to develop yourself to the highest level of personal and professional excellence. That is the price you have to pay for respect, success, equality, opportunities, and more. Overcoming racism is worth the effort; you feel accomplished only when you are successful.

You Have to Make It Happen

Do you think those who are not directly affected by racism are concerned about alleviating racism? If you want to eliminate racism in your life, you'll have to do it yourself. Because if you don't, no one else will solve your problem. You alone know what you want more than anyone else. Moreover, others are too busy going after what they want, or they may not be interested in what you want.

There are times when a situation or problem will seem impossible. But don't let that stop you any more than water going downstream will let a rock or obstacle stop it. The water keeps on moving, passing around, over, and sometimes under obstacles.

The more determined you are to overcome racism, the more you will be able to recognize opportunities to help you do just that. Have you ever wondered why you become aware of all the job opportunities in the newspaper when you are seeking employment? Somehow, becoming aware of opportunities is easy when you know what you want. Sometimes you may not find exactly what you are looking for, but you may get a lead.

Moreover, when you honestly try to succeed, people will go out of their way to help you.

First Take Care of #1

The only way to effectively help others is to first help yourself become capable of helping them. During the emergency procedures demonstration in commercial aircrafts, the flight attendants instruct passengers to put their oxygen masks on first, before putting one on a child, should the cabin pressure drop. How absolutely selfish! How can parents knowingly neglect children, especially in a life threatening situation?

Out of curiosity, I asked a stewardess why they instruct people to attend to themselves first. "You know, you are not the first one to ask me that," she said. "Children cannot take care of themselves." With a well-rehearsed smile, she continued, "incapacitated parents cannot help their children."

Often when you help people, their expectations increase. If you couldn't afford to help them in the first place, then you've put yourself in a losing situation. They are annoyed with you because you can't help them more. You are aggravated because they are unappreciative. You are annoyed with yourself for acting impulsively and jeopardizing your own position.

Be Practical

A man I know has been working on deck as an Ordinary Seaman (OS)—the lowest grade of sailor—for more than fifteen years. He currently makes about $65 per day. He constantly complains about new sailors with little experience who make more money than he. But he never complains that the wages are based on *ratings*. The higher the rating, the more money a sailor makes. The rating is achieved by having a nominal amount of sea time, successfully passing a multiple-choice exam, and sometimes, demonstrating some seamanship.

Interestingly, the company that this OS worked for bore all the cost of upgrading—classes, books, hotel, and even meals. Consistent with company policy, he was already making the maximum an OS could make. All he needed to get a raise was an upgrade to an Able-Bodied Seaman (AB). But rather than upgrade, he preferred to complain.

If you are in a dead-end situation, don't get frustrated. Look for ways to rectify the situation. If overcoming racism requires you to be the best, don't complain about being black. Become the best that you can be.

Be Willing to Start from the Bottom

If you want to rise to the top in any profession, and stay there, start from the bottom. Lower level positions are the foundation on which the entire organization rests. Employees at the lower level are often directly involved with the product(s) and/or service(s) the organization sells to the public. Can you imagine a Taco Bell without the cashier or cook? How successful would General Motors be without assembly line workers? What would happen to customer relations if bottom workers failed to satisfy the customers? Such a deficiency affects the reputation of the entire organization.

Starting from the bottom is a smart career move. Entry level positions offer many non-monetary benefits. You can obtain "hands-on" overall knowledge of the business. You often get to deal directly with the customers. You can learn what makes the organization successful or unsuccessful. You will have some ideas on making the organization more efficient. The more you understand the organization, the better you can use the system to move ahead.

Just because you start at the bottom doesn't mean that you will always be down. If you learn all about the organization and develop effective people relations, you will be well on your way to the top. There will be opportunities to move ahead. And if you prove to the world that you belong up, you shall surely rise.

Don't Hesitate to Move to the Top

There is a disproportionate number of African-Americans in low paying jobs. "The concentration of [African-Americans] in jobs paying the lowest wages," according to *The Riot Report*, "is an even more important source of [black] poverty than is outright unemployment."[2] Is racism the reason why blacks often have the jobs no one else seems to want?

There are definitely times when African-Americans cannot advance beyond the "glass ceiling." But generally, blacks get trapped in the vicious circle of low level jobs. Let's investigate some reasons which aggravate the problem:

Self-Esteem

People at the bottom are often overworked and underpaid. Moreover, they get little credit for their contributions. They often receive less respect. And they can be easily replaced. Consequently, they feel unimportant.

Fear of Responsibilities

Low self-esteem causes people to doubt their capabilities. So they feel incapable of handling supervisory responsibilities. Some people will even pass up a promotion because they are intimidated by being in control.

The Financial Trap

People who make about minimum wage have a difficult time keeping up with inflation. As they acquire more responsibilities—family, car note, mortgage payment, for example—they have to get two or more jobs just to make ends meet. Working twelve or more hours a day leaves people very little time for themselves. They don't get adequate rest, their performance deteriorates, they don't have time for personal or professional development. Consequently, their self-esteem suffers even more.

By breaking out of the vicious circle of low paying jobs, you can advance yourself personally and professionally. When you become aware of the success you are capable of, you will no longer be intimidated by racism.

The first step in breaking the circle is to decide where you want to go. Remember, no dream is too big that it cannot be realized. Next, research how you can get to where you want to be. You can talk to people who are where you want to be. Surprisingly, successful people love to tell others how they have succeeded. Your local library is a source of documented information. Librarians are often willing to help you find what you need. The rest of the journey is entirely up to you. Other African-Americans climb the ladder to success every day. You can climb to success too. There is enough room for you up there.

Either you learn to live with people, and live a prosperous life, or learn to live with the pain of great frustration and futility.

PEOPLE, WE NEED EACH OTHER

"People!" Tasha exclaimed as she slammed the phone down. Shaking her head in disgust, she began to sob.

Tasha was only 23, pretty, single, and miserable. She constantly yelled at her two children—whom she had out of wedlock—because she blamed them for "messing up" her life. One of the alleged fathers had fled; the other was married. She and her children lived with her mama. Surviving only on Food Stamps, an unofficial $100 child support, welfare and AFDC (Aid to Families with Dependent Children) checks was becoming increasingly difficult.

Her former supervisor and coworkers rejoiced when she was finally fired for misconduct, two years ago. Tasha's negative attitude and disrespect for others had polluted the work environment. She never bothered looking for another job because she always ended up getting terminated anyway.

Her only sister, who was happily married, had threatened to call the cops if Tasha ever visited her. She feared Tasha would try to break up her marriage.

Welfare had just called Tasha to inform her that they were taking legal actions against her for not reporting the child support she had been receiving.

Why was Tasha so unfortunate? Why did people treat her badly? Why did men always leave her? Why couldn't she keep a job? Tasha had a problem; a people problem. She had a negative attitude. She treated people badly and couldn't get along with anyone. As a result, Tasha brought out the worst in people. Not everyone has problems like Tasha, but you can learn a lot from her experiences with people.

Anyone can have a people problem irrespective of color, background, or social status. And the effects of poor people relations are usually detrimental. Woodrow Wilson, the 28th president, for example, considered by Dale Carnegie to be "probably the most scholarly man who ever sat in the white house," didn't know how to deal with people. Woodrow Wilson was faced with one of the greatest opportunities in history—establishing world peace. But he was unsuccessful because he couldn't handle people.[1]

Just about everything you are, everywhere you turn, everything you do often involves other people. Throughout your life—from the beginning, and probably to the end—you are in contact with people. Before you came into this world, two people—Mom and Pop—came together to make it possible. When you were a sick baby, your parents rushed you to see some people who helped you get well. You received your training and education from people. When you need groceries, you go to the store to buy from people, with money you received from other people. When you need companionship, you turn to people. How then can you live without people? Even if you could live without people, why would you want to? Considering how interdependent people are, you have to be able to get along with people.

People—your families, neighbors, coworkers, to name only a few—can bring you unimaginable happiness and fulfillment. Whether you want equality, friendship, opportunities, respect, you name it, people can give them to you. Think of times when you felt special, and you will be thinking of times when someone did something to make you feel that way. Life is dull without happiness; and without people to bring you happiness, you cannot experience joy.

Considering the amount of interaction you have with people; why aren't there more social instructions on how to deal with people? Every device you buy comes with some instructions. Why? Because you will get the most out of anything only if you understand how to handle it properly; that includes people too. If you were born with huge volumes of instructions on dealing with people, would the world be a better place? Would people have less difficulties dealing with each other? Would there be less hatred, racism and violence?

What if dealing with people is so simple that it is often overlooked? Maybe you don't need volumes of instructions. Have you ever wondered why children are usually successful in dealing with just about anyone? Why do people relationships get complicated when you grow older? Could it be that people need to return to childlike innocence in relationships? Because no matter who you are, where you come from, where you live, or what color you are, you want basically the same things that everyone else wants in life—food, shelter, safety, respect, love, acceptance, success, and more. Abraham Maslow, a behaviorist, referred to these as the needs that motivate people.

What makes people happy when they are in your company? What makes people respect you even if you are of a different race? What makes people love you? What makes them want to help you advance?

There are some basic values that people around the world have high regards for. These values are universally admired and treasured. When you have these values, you will transform enemies into lasting friends. People who see these values in your personality will not be able to stop loving you.

Here is your opportunity to find out about these values. Try incorporating these easy strategies into your day-to-day inter-action with people, and you will be surprised at how much more happiness, respect, equality, love, success, admiration, and all life's good rewards you will get from people every-where you go:

Courtesy

The Merriam-Webster Dictionary defines courtesy as "respect for others." Everyone, no matter who they are or where they come from, wants to be treated with respect. People want to feel important. According to Maslow's "pyramid of human needs," people need "respect and appreciation from others."[2] Dale Carnegie mentioned a "law" that can "almost" always keep you out of trouble if you follow it: "Always make the other person feel important."[3]

This fast-paced, stressful world has a way of cunningly rob-bing people of courtesy. When the bill collectors are ringing your phone off the hook, your landlord is threatening to evict you, you are working harder for less money, and your coworkers get quiet when you walk into the office, being cour-teous is a challenge. But never allow your hardship or situa-tion to steal away your respect for other people. If you do, you will be only reinforcing the stereotype that African-Americans are ill-mannered.

Being courteous to everyone is easy if you consider how you would feel if the situation were reversed. If you treat people how you would like to be treated, you'll have a better chance of making them happy. Remember, people like those who make them happy. People also tend to see beyond your skin color when they like you. Franklin D. Roosevelt once said: "If you treat people right, they will treat you right ninety percent of the time."

Smile

A smile is the quickest, easiest communicated, least expensive yet most precious gift you can give to everyone at virtually any time. People of every racial or ethnic group value a smile. Interestingly, a smile can also help alleviate racial stereotype. The simple act of smiling makes people feel comfortable around you. And when people are relaxed in your presence, they are more receptive; hence, they get to know the real you.

A smile can do what words cannot do; it can cross any racial, socioeconomic, or language barrier. People of every color, from every neighborhood can sense your good will when you smile with them. Even if someone doesn't know you or doesn't understand English, he/she can still relate to your smile.

Think of how you would feel around a person who smiles with you? I am not talking about that hypocritical smile either, but a genuine one. Would you feel the same way if that same person had a scowl on his/her face?

While a smile is so natural, it can be perfected. The best way to improve your smile is to practice. When you are alone, look in a mirror, and do a "before smile" and "smiling." Notice the difference? Practice smiling with yourself. Think of some pleasant experience as you smile. Don't try to force a smile; let it flow naturally. Practice, practice, practice, and in time, you will have more control over that captivating smile.

Smiling makes you look nicer; therefore, you'll feel better about yourself. That is why people ask you to smile when they take your picture. When you smile, your affirmative facial expression makes you feel positive. According to the facial feedback hypothesis,[4] facial expression stimulates the physiological response of the emotion involved.

Greetings

You enter a room and meet two people. One of them says to you: "Good morning, how are you?" The other person doesn't say a word to you. Which one of these people would you be more receptive to? If they both needed your assistance, which one would you try to help first?

Since some people have stereotyped blacks as being rude and uncultured, greeting people is effective in overcoming prejudice. Greeting people gives them the impression that you are well-mannered. You make people feel important when you greet them. People appreciate the fact that although you were not obligated to greet them, you took the time to acknowledge them. Although greeting people takes only a couple of seconds, it leaves a lasting impression of you on people's minds. Greeting people can earn you more than respect; it makes people like you. And people will go out of their way to help or understand you when they like you. Remember, when people love and respect you, they will not hate you because you are black.

You can master the art of greeting. Start by practicing being aware of people. When people are passing by you, look them in the eyes and say "hello." When you enter a car, greet the people you meet in it. When the elevator door opens, greet the people in it. When you arrive at work, greet your boss and your coworkers. You will soon see how differently people will treat you.

There are times when some people will be preoccupied, or they will feel too grumpy to reciprocate your greetings. But don't let that discourage you; say "hi" anyway. Considering how little you invest in a greeting, compared with the enormous effects it has on people, greeting everyone is a wise gesture. Go on, make someone's day; say "hello." He/she just may do the same for you.

Honesty

People in all walks of life value honesty. Paradoxically, even crooks want people to be honest with them. When people feel you are honest, there is no limit to the extent that they will trust you. They will go to great lengths to defend you if someone questions your credibility.

Honesty is a virtue in every type of relationship: family, romantic, professional, spiritual, and even casual. No amount of money can buy honesty, but the trust that honesty generates can produce millions. Honesty opens up lots of opportunities for you because people will feel that they can depend on you. With honesty, you can get all the respect you want; without honesty people turn against you quickly. Would you knowingly vote for a dishonest politician? Would you want to do business with someone who is not trustworthy?

When you are being dishonest, you emit a kind of vibration that a polygraph can detect. However, many people don't need advanced technologies to detect a lie; they can tell from your facial expression, body language, and the tone of your voice that you are being untruthful. And they may never trust you again. This could affect possible future opportunities.

Honesty is always the best policy. People are often surprisingly accommodating when you are honest with them. They may not like the situation, but they try to adapt. How many times have you heard someone say: "please, just be honest with me; I'll try to handle it"?

Because African-Americans are stereotyped as being dishonest, use every opportunity to prove that you are honest. Soon people will realize how honest you are, and they will easily trust you. The only way to alleviate the dishonest stereotype is to be honest.

Compliment

You will always meet people who impress you with their outstanding personalities. Unless you compliment people, they may not even be aware of their distinguishing assets. People of every racial or socioeconomic background love compliments. Complimenting people makes them feel special. Compliment is like fertilizer for the ego; it helps people grow. Most of all, complimenting people makes them feel that you like them. And they will interestingly start to treat you like a friend.

Here is a rule: If you admire, compliment. Think of how you feel when people tell you that they like you. Don't you feel happy when people admire your outfit? When you compliment people, you make them happy too.

Compliments stimulate conversation. Many times, if people have the time, they will tell you the story behind whatever you compliment them on. If you complimented a youth on his/her basketball skill, for example, he/she would probably say "my father showed me how to play." Through conversation, you get to know people. The more you know about people, the easier you can deal with them.

A compliment must be honest in order for it to have the positive effects intended. People don't want to be lied to. When you give people frivolous compliments, they will probably see right through you. So be genuine about your compliments.

However, because of the increased awareness of sexual harassment, a slightly offensive compliment, especially to someone of the opposite sex, could land you in lots of problems. People don't appreciate disrespect. So be considerate about your compliments. If you wanted to compliment someone, for example, instead of: "baby, you look so hot," a simple "your dress is very pretty," or "your suit looks good on you," will be well-appreciated.

Like everything else, compliments lose their impact when you overuse them on one person. Be selective and sincere. As a general rule, don't overuse compliments, especially not on the same person. People feel you are trying to "kiss up" to them when you over-compliment them. And they will lose respect for you. Compliments will help alleviate racism only if you use them to improve your relationship with people.

Reliability

It is fifteen minutes past your quitting time. You have been standing for eight hours. Your relief still has not shown up.

At home, you sit by the phone for hours, waiting and hoping that special person will call like he/she promised.

You are a little worried about getting to work tomorrow morning. Even though your neighbor has promised to give you a ride, you're not sure if she will forget about you again.

None of the preceding examples is desirable, but they happen, because some people are not reliable. Being unreliable turns people against you quickly. People lose respect for you when you disappoint them. Would you want a coworker who is always late or doesn't do his/her share of the work? Would you use a garage that doesn't have your car ready when you were told to pick it up? Most likely not.

If someone does not live up to his/her responsibilities, some innocent person will have to pick up the slack. Sometimes, things don't get done, schedules go haywire, and people are needlessly affected.

Because blacks are stereotyped as being unreliable, you can overcome racism by being reliable. To earn the rewarding reputation of being reliable, always try to stick to schedules. If you are slow, get a head start. Set your watch a couple of minutes ahead if you have to. Plan well in advance. However, if something goes wrong, like it sometimes does, call and let someone know that you will be late. There are phones at almost every filling station and around the streets. If you don't have a quarter, call collect.

Interest in Others

People love those who show interest in them. Who are some of the people you like the most? Why do you like them? Have you noticed that other people like them also? When you become interested in other people and treat them well, they just can't help but love you, no matter what color you are.

If you observe popular politicians' habits, you'll discover that they all have one thing in common: they are interested in their constituents. The most loved politicians always try to make people happy, give them hope, and improve their lives. They don't deceive their constituents just to get elected. Although, you may not be interested in a political office, you can adapt the charisma of influential politicians. You can learn to tell people what they want to hear; do what they expect of you; show them that you care about them; and help them whenever you can.

In *How to Win Friends and Influence People*, Dale Carnegie concluded the chapter "Six Ways to Make People Like You" with the following: "If you want others to like you, if you want to develop real friendship, if you want to help others at the same time help yourself, . . . Become genuinely interested in other people."[5]

When you become interested in people, you'll understand them better, and enjoy relationships. Why? Because you will start to see things from their perspective, understand why they discriminate, and get a sense of their insecurities.

When you show interest in others, believe it or not, you will become popular and in demand, almost overnight. You will feel better about yourself when you realize how important you really are. Moreover, you will feel happy when you make other people happy. Every quality you develop or enhance that positively influences people, helps you overcome discrimination.

Recommended Readings

1. Carnegie, Dale. How to Win Friends and Influence People. Rev. ed. New York: Simon, 1981.

2. Gabor, Don. How to Start a Conversation and Make Friends. New York: Fireside, 1983.

*Your self-control cannot be destroyed if you
don't want it to be.*

HANDLING NEGATIVE PEOPLE

*Swabbing the sweat from his forehead, Ike turned to Ernest.
"Man!" shaking his head, "Chipping rust in all this heat; we can do
better than this."*

"You can go flip burgers, but I'm staying," Ernest replied defensively. "This is a good job."

*"Flip burgers?" Ike admonished as he stood on top of the empty
milk crate. Ike pushed up his chest as he saluted the calm seas. "I
want to be a captain," he said.*

*"A captain, huh?" Ernest asked sarcastically as he continued chipping away at the deck of the tugboat. "Don't waste your time, bro,
you're black."*

*"I can't believe you," Ike said. "But thanks for the advice anyway,
BROTHER."*

"You're very welcome," Ernest replied with a grin, feeling satisfied he had once again talked some sense into Ike.

*About two years had passed, and Ernest was scheduled to go back
to the same tugboat he and Ike had been on together—crew members
were assigned to boats at random. Guess who Ernest met again? Ike.
Only this time, Ike was no longer a deckhand, but a mate (second in
command).*

Negative people—those who tell you what you cannot become; those who try to discourage you; those who are always bitter about other people and life in general—are everywhere. Negative people are not only limited to racist groups, they can be other blacks, your next-door neighbors, coworkers, or even your immediate family members.

Dealing with Negative People

You cannot run away from negative people; they are everywhere. Unless you know how to handle negative people, they will make you miserable.

The following strategies will make dealing with any negative person a positive experience:

Control the Negative in You

We all periodically have our outburst of negative attitudes, especially when we don't get our way. Being bitter makes you and anyone around you unhappy. Think of how you feel around a person who is being ugly. Others are alienated when you are being negative. You probably can recall times when you said or did something negative to hurt someone. Did your action make you happy? Did your relationship with the person you hurt ever return to normal? Being negative is disadvantageous to everyone and must be prevented.

Overcoming racism requires you to control your negative emotions. How? By shifting your focus from the problem to possible solutions, you can avoid much frustration. If someone tells you that you are not qualified for your job, don't get mad. Don't feel hurt either. Instead, look for ways to prove to the whole world that you are the most qualified person for that job.

If your tire went flat while driving to your family reunion, would you cry, kick the car, and curse the flat tire? Would you scream at other cars and wish they all had flat tires? Would being bitter get you to your reunion? Certainly not. Just as you would try to change the tire, or get assistance, you should try to find solutions to any problem that pops up.

Planning is most effective against problems. Although you don't know the future, you can establish contingencies for possible problems. Let's go back to the flat tire example. If you had put a spare tire in your trunk, you wouldn't have to worry about getting a tow truck. You could change the tire in less than half an hour and be on your way.

Don't Let Negative People Affect You

Negative people will make you miserable if you let them. If people don't have control over their situation, they have a problem, not you. So why get upset with people who cannot control their negative emotions? Just because a racist wants to feel superior by trying to humiliate you doesn't mean that you should feel inferior. If negative people had any control over their emotions, they wouldn't let pessimism tarnish their personalities. Negative people definitely have problems; don't let them make their problems yours.

H. Norman Wright, a professor of counseling, wrote the following about negative people:

> They are afraid to take risks on new ideas. They struggle with disappointments. They don't want to risk failures, so they oppose any opportunity where failure is a possibility. They see themselves as lacking control over their lives, so negativism is their way of expressing control. Unfortunately, the negativists' eagerness to control their own lives leads them to control other people in the process, making them difficult to be around.[1]

In dealing with negative people, you can do one or more of the following: tell negative people frankly what they are doing; they may not be aware of their actions. Ask them why they are being so negative; they may need someone to reach out to them. How many times have you heard, "he is not that bad," or "she just needs a little getting used to"? Walk away from a negative situation; being defensive only escalates the problem. According to a *Reader's Digest* article, "sarcasm will never work (the [negative] person will interpret it as an invitation to fight harder)."[2]

When dealing with negative people, never allow yourself to lose control. Negative people will try hard to prove that they are not the only ones who do not have control over themselves. Losing control of yourself can lead to an argument or a fight. You don't deserve to sink to their level.

When you exhibit control over yourself, you feel a sense of power. Because you are not letting pathetic people control your emotions, you are victorious. Negative people, on the contrary, feel like losers because they cannot make you act the way they want you to. They will admire your strength. Often, people return to apologize for their negativism. How often have you heard, "look, man, I'm sorry about the way I acted; I don't know what got into me"?

Never Try to Change Negative People

A negative person can be more defiant than a rebellious teenager. Trying to change negative people is more frustrating than it's worth. Moreover, people tend to become resentful when you try to change them. You cannot change negative people; they have to change themselves. However, the most effective way to help negative people improve is to maintain control of your emotions. Show negative people that having a positive attitude is possible. Let them see that their efforts to frustrate you are useless. Give them a reason to want to be like you.

Below all the negativism are insecure people. They are afraid to get hurt, so they are paranoid. Be patient with them. Love them if you can. Be nice to them although they are awful. You could be a major instrument in bringing joy to painful souls. You have nothing to lose. When you give love, you feel spiritually rewarded. When negative people receive your love, their lives become fulfilled.

Good luck and love the world. Don't leave yourself out though.

Recommended Reading

1. Wright, H. Norman. <u>How to Get Along with Almost Anyone</u>. Dallas: Word, 1989.

Most invaluable things in life are free or cost little, compared with their benefits.

INFORMATION: THE KEY TO POSSIBILITIES

Every day, people of every ethnic group—blacks, whites, Hispanics, Asians—are making the amount of money you would like to be making; some people are doing what you would like to be doing; others are accomplishing what you only dream about. What is so special about people who get what they want? The answer is simple. Successful people know how to succeed. With the "right" information anyone can achieve anything. If other people can be successful, you can be successful too, if only you knew how.

With pertinent information, the seemingly "complex" task is easy. Information can guide you through various levels of accomplishments. Even if you never attended cooking classes, at least not formally, with the right recipe as your guide, you could prepare a gourmet meal. If you have any doubt, try out a recipe and make dinner for the family tonight.

Detailed Information

The more detail you have, the easier you can accomplish your goal. Detail helps you to efficiently plan, prevent costly mistakes, monitor your progress, to name a few.

Let's use the following scenario as an example: You urgently need some important documents from your manager, who is stuck at home nursing the flu. The documents are too sensitive to send by just anyone. So, you have to pick them up. Anyway, your manager gives you directions to her place. Which directions would be more effective?

"Get off I-10 on the Causeway exit. Take the service road. Turn on Division Street. My address is 2504 Division, apt. 20001."

or

"Take I-10 East, get off on Exit #229A. Take Causeway South. There is a Time Saver on the right. Turn right at the first traffic light, onto the service road and continue for about a mile. You will see three tall buildings. The first is a medical college. At the third building which is gray, turn left on Division Street. Come down Division past Ripplesquare Apartments. The next apartment complex is Madison Garden. Turn right into the first driveway. The building you'll see is `D.' My apartment is #20001, the third on the right from the front entrance."

Obviously the latter directions are more detailed and easier to follow.

Information Is at Your Disposal

There is information on practically every subject of interest: becoming rich, technologies, sciences, law, education, music, medicine, and much more. Whether you want to overcome racism, become a billionaire, manage an aircraft plant, become a better basketball player, get financial aid, become a better lover, or satisfy your curiosity, there is information available to help you.

There is some sensitive information accessible by only a selected few—intelligence and investigation agents, for example—because it is confidential. Such information is often useless to the public anyway. However, there is so much useful information attainable by virtually anyone.

Why let racism hinder your progress when you can overcome racism? Why struggle from paycheck to paycheck when you can have more money than you need? Why drive that jalopy when you can ride in a classic automobile? You could afford your dream home. You can help as many people as you want. Some African-Americans enjoy enormous success. You can be successful too.

The secrets to success are not classified; they are accessible by anyone. Success secrets are yours for the taking. But where do you find them?

Start with Your Local Library

Your local library is a source of valuable information. A large library can be compared with a super store. Like a super store, the library offers a variety of products and services under one roof: books on various topics, magazines, references, maps, video tapes, cassettes, compact discs, computers, research assistance, access via modem to libraries and collections all over the world, and much more. Whether you need to get out of a dead end job, want a promotion, are interested in starting your own business, need help preparing your taxes, for example, your library can help you.

It is easy to become overwhelmed by all the information in the library. But don't get intimidated any more than you would allow a super store to frighten you. Library cataloging systems enable you to easily find various products and services. Catalog cards or computerized catalogs give you the exact location of your subject of interest. You can access books by subject, title, author, category, or call number, for example.

If you were interested in starting a home business, you would go into subject on the computer and type in "home business." The computer will give you a list, description, and location of all the information on home businesses. You will get, for example, information on starting a home business, tax laws for home businesses, statistics on success or failure of home businesses, and being a successful entrepreneur.

Like super stores, libraries are staffed with helpful employees. Librarians are well-informed people who will help you to find the information you need. Unlike super stores that can cost you an entire paycheck, libraries are usually free or inexpensive. Many libraries have free membership which might entitle you to check out books, magazines, video tapes, CDs, or order material from other libraries and research services through interlibrary loan.

Getting the Most out of Your Library

Use the main branch of your local library whenever you can. Main branches often have a wider range of information and services compared with smaller branches.

Treat library staff with respect. Ask librarians for help whenever you need to; they are there to assist you. The information you need for success in solving your problems is there; you simply have to learn to find it.

Get in Touch with Associations

People with similar interests join like "birds of a feather flock together." If you have an interest, chances are there's an association out there for you. There are several thousand associations for just about every imaginable interest nationwide: National Minority Business Council, National Council of African-American Men, Negro Airmen International, Calorie Control Council, National Council of Black Faculty, S.C.O.R.E. (Service Corps of Retired Executives), which offers free professional advise on starting and operating small businesses, and there is even the Beer Can Collectors of America.

You can find a listing of associations in the *Encyclopedia of Associations*, a multivolume reference, published by Gale, and found in most libraries. The *Black Americans Information Directory*, a reference also published by Gale, is another source of information on African-American organizations, fellowships, businesses, studies, scholarships, loan programs, and more. Scan through these references whenever you are in a library; you will be amazed by all the opportunities available. If you have access to the internet, you can also find active interest groups online.

People in associations have varying degrees of experience and expertise. You can learn much from association members; many of them will relate to you because they have been where you now are, a novice.

Associations can help you advance much faster because they are a source of valuable pertinent information, professional support, and to some extent, moral and emotional support. I've always employed the services of associations. My most prominent experience with associations was with the Aircraft Owners and Pilots Association (AOPA). When I was a midshipman at a military college, I realized, during my sophomore year, that my long held dream of flying was persistent. I wanted to be a pilot so badly, but I could not afford flying lessons. Being a full-time student on a scholarship, I barely earned $20 per week from odd jobs around campus. Flying lessons were too expensive a hobby for me. Anyway, I contacted AOPA and became a member.

For an annual membership fee of $39, I borrowed enough money, at a very low interest rate, to finance my flight training from Private to Commercial Pilot. My AOPA membership also entitled me to toll-free flight planning assistance, discounted aeronautical charts, discounted aircraft and car rentals, medical advice on matters relating to Federal Aviation Administration (FAA) medical certification, flight and legal insurance, online services, airport and weather data, a monthly subscription to *AOPA Pilot* magazine, and so much more.

Associations gain more influence and profitability when they expand. And there is no better way to expand than to recruit new members, which means you. Associations often hold classes, seminars, or meetings that will aid you in becoming better at the organization's objective.

Most associations charge a nominal membership fee. The membership fees vary with associations. The advantages of associations often far exceed the membership cost. However, before you commit to an association, find out all you can about the association. Ascertain that the association offers what you need to achieve your goal.

Map out Your Plan

The most pertinent information is beneficial only if you use it. You need a plan to effectively use information, a plan that is practical and fits your individual needs.

In devising your plan, seek help from professionals whenever necessary. People with experience in your area of interest can offer invaluable guidance. Hotlines, associations, and support groups are often staffed by knowledgeable employees who offer free counseling or they may charge a nominal fee. Many associations even have toll free numbers.

With a desire to overcome racism coupled with pertinent information, success is only a matter of time.

Recommended Reading

1. Berkman, Robert I. <u>Find It Fast</u>. New York: Harper, 1987.

You can learn to go as far as you want.

EDUCATION: A REAL NECESSITY

"Miss Joyce?" the squeaky voice echoed out of the intercom. "The president would like to see you in his office."

"Ok, I'll be there in five minutes," Joyce replied as she fumbled through stacks of computer printouts on her desk.

"Hummm . . . , he wants to see you right now," the secretary said. "He and Mr. Hudson are waiting for you."

"OK, thanks, I'll be right over."

Joyce got concerned. Their shipyard hadn't had a new contract for several months. There wasn't any job pending either. She wondered why the president of the company and her immediate boss wanted to see her right away. A scary thought flashed across her mind, but she quickly dispelled it. "I've been here too long; besides, I'm a black woman, they wouldn't fire me."

The president's door was ajar when Joyce arrived. "Please come in, Miss Joyce," the president called out. Motioning her to sit in the large couch directly in front of his neatly organized desk, he continued. "Please have a seat."

"Why is he being so polite?" Joyce thought. "I really don't like this."

"Miss Joyce," the president said. "You have been a dedicated employee since you started with us ten years ago." He paused again. "However, we no longer need your service."

Joyce couldn't believe what she had just heard. For a brief moment, everything in the room seemed dark. She secretly hoped the president was joking. But she knew better.

"But why?" she choked. Her eyes were already red with anger and frustration. Feeling empty, she silently waged an unsuccessful war against her tears.

There was silence for a few seconds. Her boss, sitting in front of the president's desk, took the opportunity to answer. "Miss Joyce, you have failed to develop professionally to help make the company competitive."

"I don't get it," Joyce calmly replied. "I have ten years of experience with this company."

"No, Miss Joyce," her boss answered, shaking his head, "you have about one year of experience ten times. The shipbuilding industry is not like it used to be ten years ago. We have a company to run. We have to be competitive just to remain in business. We need someone who can do the job."

Joyce knew he was right. When she started working here, she never imagined the shipbuilding industry would change so drastically. She had always felt a sense of job security.

The Pink Slip Trend

Many companies, large and small, continue to lay people off. A *Newsweek* article reported ". . . giant companies are still shedding workers by the tens of thousands, . . . no one seems immune."[1] Even the federal government is laying people off and closing down some military installations.

There were times when people working for the government or major companies—Boeing, IBM, and AT&T, for example—may have felt their professional future was secured. But do people have job security today? Seventy percent of employees who didn't get laid off, from 909 companies surveyed, expressed job insecurity, according to a *U.S. News & World Report* article.[2]

Fierce domestic and foreign competition is causing companies to "streamline." Survival for many companies today means cutting expenses by consolidating departments, closing down unprofitable business units, investing in more efficient people and equipment, and worst of all, laying off "excess" employees.

Let's take the automobile industry, for example. Do you remember the days when Ford, Chrysler, and General Motors were the leading car manufacturers in the United States? What is happening to American cars today? The automobile market is flooded with cars from all over the world. *The World Almanac and Book of Facts 1995* listed the Honda Accord, for example, as the top-selling passenger car in the United States, for two consecutive years.[3] Who would have thought that cars like the Toyota Camry, Nissan Altima, Honda Civic, and other foreign cars would outsell American cars? Why did these cars become so popular? Can American automobile manufacturers still afford to maintain all their employees?

Consumers Are Savvy

Consumers are critical about what they spend their hard-earned money on. People want the best their money can buy—quality products and friendly efficient services. Consumers are willing to patronize whoever satisfies their needs.

Let's take you, for example. Suppose you were going out to shop for a car; what would be your two most basic requirements? If you want an affordable and reliable automobile, you are not alone. Many people are busy with their daily chores; they don't have time nor the money to keep taking a car back to the dealership for something that could have been done right the first time.

What Downsizing Means to African-Americans

An *Ebony* article stated that: "Although whites and other minorities lost and found jobs," according to a study, "blacks were the only group to lose more positions than they gained."[4] Why are African-Americans increasingly vulnerable to possible lay offs?

• Some folks still believe that blacks are intellectually inferior, hence, professionally incapable. Prejudice causes many people to think that African-Americans are only in high-level positions to fulfill quotas. So when the opportunity to cut back arises, guess who gets the pink slip first?

• Corporations can now legally fulfill their equal employment requirements by reporting minority employees as one group. This means that corporations can replace African-Americans with other "preferred" minorities.

• Asians, Hispanics, Native Americans, and other minorities are still preferred to blacks. A University of Chicago study, in 1988, indicated that "blacks are more segregated than any other race."[5]

• Blacks are stereotyped as been irrational. Some managements perceive getting rid of African-Americans as a proactive measure to prevent possible problems.[6]

You Have to Be the Best

Overcoming racism is the only solution to racial prejudice. African-Americans must rise above racism because ". . . when America catches a cold, Black America gets a flu." Claudette Sims wrote in *Don't Weep for Me*: "When America gets hypertension, Black America has a stroke."[7] The bottom line is, blacks have to be the best. But how? By learning to overcome racism.

Education is the perfect path towards alleviating any form of social oppression. Therefore, you should strive to learn as much as possible. When you take advantage of educational opportunities, you personally benefit. Moreover, your family, friends, community, state, and country reap the rewards of having a well-informed citizen. You become capable of analyzing and improving deteriorating race relations. Your salary increases. You will be able to afford the goods and services that you want. You will have more job security because companies will not want to part with a productive employee.

If you do not learn to overcome racism, you can expect to continue to be treated like a second-class citizen. That is just the way the situation is, but that is not how it should be. You can make a difference. The improvements you make in your own professional value help you, me, and all African-Americans.

Don't Be Afraid of Education

If the thought of education intimidates you, don't feel helpless; many people feel uneasy about learning. Although education will make you more marketable, there's a tendency to get terrified about going back to school. You may feel that getting back into the school routine, after being out of school for awhile, will be difficult. Or, you may feel that traditional aged students will reject you. You may think of many other reasons not to return to school.

You are already too busy with work and raising children. You may worry about paying your bills, when you are a full-time student with no source of regular income. Or you may get petrified at the thought of fighting to stay awake as some soft spoken monotone professor babbles on for hours about some boring subject. But no matter what your fear about education is, it is valid. The idea of school is scary; but so is the realization that you are doomed to the agony of racism if you do not overcome job discrimination through continuing education and training.

Don't Put All the Blame on Yourself

"I'm not good in math." "I never was good in school." "I'm not smart." "School just isn't for me." These are common degrading comments people make about their academic performance. But before you belittle yourself, stop to consider that maybe a poor academic performance is not all your fault.

The effectiveness of teachers plays a major role in your perception of education. What were some of your favorite classes? Did you enjoy those classes because the teachers made the subjects interesting?

Competent teachers come to class prepared; they are knowledgeable and they know how to effectively relay information to their students. Good teachers make even the most boring subject interesting; they know how to hold their students' attention. Good teachers stimulate their students' imaginations by creating suspense. The students become curious to learn more. As a result of having professional teachers, learning becomes exciting.

Incompetent teachers can make the best subject uninteresting. Some ineffective teachers are knowledgeable, but they are poor communicators. Consequently, perplexed students lose interest in education.

A teacher can be compared with a movie. When the movie is interesting, you are on your toes, carefully studying each scene. When the movie is long over, you may even remember almost everything that happened. You may be able to recite some of the dialogue. Whereas, when the movie is boring, you probably wouldn't even remember the end. When you start to lose interest, your mind immediately begins to wander. And, the movie is over for you long before it even ends.

Unless you are paying attention, it is difficult to remember anything. Unless the teacher captures your attention by making the subject interesting, learning can be a bore. However, you can learn to make the best of a "boring" education.

Kick Any Potential Fear or Boredom out of Education

You cannot enjoy and benefit from education if it scares or bores you. Amidst the mounting violence in public schools and the mostly overworked and underpaid teachers, you can still get an education if you really want to.

Education can be a beneficial and enjoyable experience if you use the following strategies:

Go for a Discipline That Interests You

If you like a subject, your interest will take the "chore" out of studying. As a result, you will learn more.

Try to Conceive the Opportunities Education Can Open up for You

Education does more than make you well-informed, it can lead to valuable *networking*. Your schoolmates, professors, alumni, and others, are all sources of potential references. Your professor could recommend you for an ideal job. Your classmate may have some contacts at the company you want to work for. Remember, people are apt to recommend those that they personally know.

Education improves your chances of financial security by making you marketable. People with four or more years of college, in 1991 for example, had the lowest unemployment rate, only three percent. Whereas, people with about one to three years of high school, had the highest rate, 14.8%.[8]

Get the Most out of Your Education

If you wanted to get to the top of the Empire State Building, you could climb 1575 steps or you could take the elevator. If anything can be done fast and efficiently, why torture yourself by using more effort than necessary?

Time is much too expensive, and money is too valuable to waste on anything that you don't benefit from. Getting the most out of your education makes every second and every penny you invest worth the investment. Moreover, education enables you to disprove the stereotype that African-Americans are intellectually inferior.

Here are some easy strategies to help make your trip to the top of any educational height a success:

Get a Head Start

If you are slow, which you'll most likely be in the beginning, get a head start. In just about every class, the teacher often gives students a copy of the syllabus (a list of topics to be covered), at the beginning. For some seminars, and special classes, you may get the syllabus earlier.

Familiarize yourself with topics that will be covered. The library can help you. Or if you know someone who attended the class, pick his/her brain. Ask him/her about the class and teacher.

Ask Questions

How many times has another student asked the same question you had wanted to ask the teacher? When you are not comprehending a part of a lecture, chances are, other students may be having difficulties understanding too. When you ask a question, other students may also benefit, like you sometimes benefit from their questions.

Many teaches are willing to entertain questions. Some teachers will even tell you to "raise your hand," if you have a question. Questions do more than get answers: they serve as a feedback for the teacher. Many teachers can evaluate the effectiveness of their lecture by the number of questions students ask.

Never be afraid to ask questions because you feel that other students may think you are stupid. An old calculus professor of mine used to say: "The only stupid question is the one that you don't ask." If you don't understand, ask for help. If you don't let the teacher know that you are having problems, he/she may believe that you understood the lecture. You will not be deceiving the teacher; you will be deceiving yourself. Your confusion will become obvious during exams.

If you feel that asking questions will slow down the lecture, at least write the question down and ask the teacher right after class. Many times, your question will be answered before the session is over. However, if your question wasn't covered, meet the teacher at a "suitable" time. The best time to approach a teacher is when he/she is preparing to go on to the next class. Put the old courtesy to work for you. Almost no teacher will resist the: "Excuse me, I didn't quite understand so and so, can you please go over it with me?" If the teacher is running out of time, he/she will often set up an appointment with you.

Seek Help from Your Fellow Students

In every class, there always seems to be some students who catch on faster than others. Are they geniuses? Beats me! The more someone can relate to what is being taught, the easier he/she comprehends. If your mom worked in the emergency room of the local hospital and you visited her often, you would probably relate to trauma lectures in your first aid class. Would you be able to relate to physics the same way? Most likely if your dad is a physicist.

Some of these "smart" kids may flaunt their knowledge by trying to answer every question the teacher asks. That's good for them. If they want to show off, they probably will not hesitate to spend a couple of minutes helping you with your studies. You may be able to understand fellow students better than you can a teacher.

Your knowledgeable classmates will benefit by helping you with your studies. They will have the opportunity to exhibit their brilliance. Moreover, you can acquire knowledge that will always be yours. You will be able to use your understanding to get ahead.

Take Notes

It is always helpful to take thorough, clear notes. Even if the teacher distributes notes, make your own notes. You don't have to write down every word the teacher utters, just write down the main points, and some explanations. The key to effective note-taking is to write down anything that helps you remember.

You can also highlight important points in your book that the teacher emphasizes. Many teachers draw exam questions from points they emphasized in class.

When I had a spelling problem in elementary school, a teacher gave me a remedy: "If you want to remember a word, write it down." Anyway, that teacher's advice was also valuable in college—especially for remembering those complex organic chemistry and calculus formulas—and in graduate school.

Writing something down actually demands your attention. And you tend to remember what you pay attention to. Have you noticed that you remember a phone message, for example, if you write the message down?

Some students find recording a lecture much easier than writing notes. Taped lectures can be reviewed as often as necessary. You also remember what you repeatedly hear. You can buy an inexpensive pocket sized tape recorder for classes.

Always get permission from the teacher before taping his/her lecture. Many teachers will not mind, but as a rule, ask first.

Follow Up

The end of class doesn't mean the end of studies. Use those boring moments to go over your notes while they are still fresh in your mind. Read your notes or listen to your taped lectures as often as necessary. Look for books or articles that deal with what you are studying. The objective is to help yourself relate to the subject more. The more points of view you have the better; one perspective just may "click."

Studying is almost entirely up to you. No amount of instruction can replace studying. The more devoted you are, the more you will achieve. Don't get frustrated if you are having difficulty comprehending a topic. Some subjects require a little more time than others. Make a note of your problems and get someone to help you.

Education is power; the power to succeed. There is no better way to disprove the racial stereotype that blacks are stupid than to become educated. You are never too old or too young to learn. Moreover, whatever you learn is yours. No one can take your education away from you. I'll close this chapter with the words of William Hazlitt: "Learning is its own exceeding great reward."

*Time is the one thing you and everyone else
has an equal amount of.*

TIME: YOUR MOST VALUABLE MEDIUM OF EXCHANGE

Everyone—blacks, whites, Hispanics, Native Americans, Arabs—has an equal amount of time. How you use your twenty-four hours each day determines how successful or unsuccessful you are. No matter how rich or poor you are, time is still one of your most valuable assets.

You eventually trade time for just about everything you get in life. You put in those hours to get that paycheck. If you are on welfare, you had to spend time filling out the thirty or more pages of questionnaire, and going through the bureaucratic procedures. If you want to raise children, you have to spend time nurturing them.

If you don't exchange time for what you want, you do not accomplish your desire; moreover, some unpleasant repercussion could occur. Can you imagine what would happen to the relationship with your loved ones if you didn't spend time with them? Your spouse could feel abandoned. Your children could feel neglected. Even when you are sick, you have to spend time at the hospital seeing the doctor, undergoing treatment, and resting; all in exchange for a hopeful recovery. You feel gratified when your time is well-spent. Think of a time in your life when you did something that made you proud, and you will be thinking of time that was spent well. If you don't use your time efficiently, you lose it.

The Law of Demand and Availability

Would you buy water for $20,000? You need water to survive. But you probably wouldn't hesitate to buy a new Cadillac for twenty-grand. You can live comfortably without owning a car. So why would you be willing to spend more on an automobile than you would spend on water? Because water is readily available. You get water when you turn on the faucet. The rain brings water. About seventy-five percent of the Earth's surface is covered with water.

People will spend more money on a product or service they want, provided the product or service is not readily available. When you have a superior product or if you can perform a task better than anyone else, people will be willing to pay more money for your time investment. Your time becomes valuable when it is in demand; therefore, you feel important. And whenever you feel good about yourself, you are overcoming racism.

The Real Value of Time

A dollar is a dollar. A dollar may buy a little more, sometimes a little less, depending on inflation, but it can never be more than a dollar. Whereas, every minute of your time is as valuable as you make it. A minute could be used to save a life or help another person. A minute could even be used to drink a cup of coffee.

Time is too valuable to waste. Use your time to succeed and overcome racism. I like Bernard Berenson's humorous saying about time: "I would willingly stand at street corners, hat in hand, begging passersby to drop their unused minutes into it."

Time Has Its Drawback

Time indiscriminately waits for no one; it keeps on moving. Once you missed a particular time, it's gone forever. You may be able to do what you miss in the future, but there's no guarantee. The only time actually guaranteed is now, so use the moment wisely.

Every single minute of your time is an opportunity to do something worthwhile. Here's what the late Dr. Martin Luther King, Jr. said about using your time: "We must use time creatively . . . and forever realize that the time is always ripe to do right."

If you do what is supposed to be done, now, you will hopefully have time reserved—like money in the bank—to use later for other projects.

Make Your Time More Valuable

If you want respect and equality, you have to prove to the world that you deserve them. By being the best in the areas that are in demand in our society, you can overcome negative racial stereotype. Becoming the best in any endeavor requires you to invest your time in acquiring knowledge, training, experience, and more. But you must have control over your time in order to utilize it efficiently.

You will gain greater control over your time by breaking up your daily activities into manageable parts. Here are some easy strategies to help you develop effective time management:

Take an Inventory of Your Time

Taking inventory is crucial; you already inventory your time several times during the day. When you are commuting to work, you check your watch to see how much more time you have. During your coffee break, you frequently check your time. When you are expecting a friend at a certain time, you monitor your watch to see how much longer before your friend will show up.

In your personal notebook, make a list of what you do with your 24 hours, on the average, each day. The times don't have to be exact to the minute; an approximation will work just fine. Make sure your list includes but is not limited to the following: sleep, work, commuting, eating, breaks, cleaning, etc.

A typical list may look like this:

INVENTORY OF TWENTY-FOUR HOURS		
Events	**Hrs.**	**Mins.**
Sleep - - - - - - - - - - - - - - -	8	
Bath - - - - - - - - - - - - - - -		15
Dressing - - - - - - - - - - - - -		10
Breakfast - - - - - - - - - - - -		6
Commuting to work - - - - -		35
Work - - - - - - - - - - - - - -	8	
Coffee break - - - - - - - - - -		15
Lunch break - - - - - - - - - -	1	
Commuting back home - - -		40
Dinner - - - - - - - - - - - - -		30
TV - - - - - - - - - - - - - - - -	4	
Preparing for next day - - -		30
Preparing for bed - - - - - -		20
Total	24 H	21 M

Whoops, "so much to do; so little time." Many people will have a lot more to do than what's on the list. It is not unusual for some people to have about 36 hours of things to do in 24 hours.

The question is: How do you manage with only 24 hours? And the answer is: Do the best you can. Professor Northcote Parkinson, an author, believed that "work expands to fill the time available for its completion." So, by allocating less time to perform a task, you can get a lot done in 24 hours.

Make a "To Do" List

A list of your activities can help you make more efficient use of your time. A list reminds you of what you need to do, what you have already done, keeps you on track, and even saves you time. Let's use the grocery store example again. (If you are thinking that I like the grocery store example a lot, you are partly right; I like what's in the grocery store—food.) Have you ever tried grocery shopping without the list that you forgot on the kitchen table at home? You probably had to walk through each aisle scanning to see if something on the shelves reminded you of what you needed. After all the time wasted, you still may have forgotten to pick up the sweet potatoes. Whereas, if you had your list, you could just go to the appropriate aisle to pick up what you wanted. Not only do you save time using a list, you spare frustration as well.

Don't worry about adding items to your "To Do" list; put as many items on it as you can. Your goal should be completing your list. However, you must strive to complete those items that are most important, so prioritize. Whatever you can't finish today can be done tomorrow. But be careful to guard against procrastination. At least you will feel a sense of accomplishment after doing the crucial items on your list. As you scratch off items on your list, you become reassured of your progress.

Budget Time to Take Action

Nothing gets done unless someone does it. The longest list, detailed planning, and motivation are effective only if you take action. If you can get a task done now, why wait until later? I like what Alexander Woollcott had to say about taking action: "Many of us spend half our time wishing for things we could have if we didn't spend half our time wishing."

When you are accomplishing a certain task, try to minimize any distraction. Focus on what you are doing at the time. If you can afford to put everything else off, do so. If you get an interrupting phone call or an unexpected visitor, for example, be brief with the distractions. If necessary, tell your visitor that you will be with him/her later. If you let your visitor know how important your task is, he/she may even offer to help you.

Budget Time for Personal Development

Try to set some time aside for developing yourself. The time can be spent reading an inspirational book, watching an informative program, taking a special class at your community college, or practicing a sport. Any activity that can help you feel better about yourself enables you to overcome racism.

Any time can be used for personal development, but the best time is early in the morning or late in the evening. Waking up a couple of minutes earlier, if you are a morning person, or going to bed later, if you are a night person, will give you some extra time for personal development.

Budget Time to Review

Every experience is an opportunity to gain some valuable knowledge. "Experience is the best teacher"; you can learn a lot from it. At the conclusion of an important event, like after a meeting, a class, a fight with your friend, or even at the end of the day, take a few minutes to reflect on what happened. What was good about the situation(s)? What made the outcome favorable, and what could you have done to make things better? What was frustrating? The more you learn from these little review sessions, the more you will be able to make your next experience beneficial.

Review can also be especially helpful when you are faced with a problem. Instead of acting on impulse, stop and ask yourself what can make the outcome more favorable. How can you prevent the situation from becoming a problem? A few seconds of reflection can save you lots of possible frustration, loses, and money.

Budget Time to Plan

Planning is essential in almost every situation. Even if you are experienced in a particular task, planning can help; if you are inexperienced, planning is more critical. Planning need not be a tedious, down to the minute detail task. Planning can be a momentary reflection on how you wish to accomplish your goal.

Asking yourself the following will make planning easier: What do I want to accomplish? How can it be done? How can I succeed? When is the best time to succeed? You can come up with as many questions as you deem necessary to build a good game plan.

Because situations can be unpredictable, always keep your plan flexible. Don't hesitate to adjust your plan when the need arises. Trying to keep to a rigid plan would be like holding your steering wheel in only one position as you drive down the interstate. You have to keep making directional adjustments to reach your destination.

Budget Time for Breaks

Have you noticed how ineffective a sponge gets when it's saturated with water? A sponge can absorb only so much water before becoming full. Squeeze the water out of the sponge and it is ready to absorb more. You are like a sponge in many respects; you can function well up to a point, before you start to become bored, tired, aggravated, and possibly lose interest and attention. Your productivity suffers as a result, sometimes with some potentially devastating results.

How effective would you be, for example, driving a 500-mile trip without a break? A break can rejuvenate you. Remember the boost you sometimes feel to tackle a task right after a little break? The amount of effort you put into a task before needing a break will vary from task to task. Pay attention to your physiological and psychological reactions; you alone know how much you can tolerate.

A break doesn't necessarily have to be a long period of rest; it can be as brief as momentarily switching to a different task. A break could be pulling to the side of the road and getting out of the car to stretch your legs, for example.

No matter what kind of break you take, a break allows you to regenerate attention. The result you achieve after a slight break will more than make up for a momentary neglect of a task. A break could even save your life.

Budget Time to Play

Hard work and achievements are fine, but every now and then you will need time off to play; it is essential for your well-being. Playing doesn't necessarily mean jumping up and down like some child, it can be a game of basketball, exercising, aerobics, dancing, and many other physically and mentally stimulating activities.

Playing can help you laugh and have fun. Playing is a good remedy for stress because it takes you away from work, for a while.

Budget Time for Companionship

You need other people. People are a source of happiness, support, advice, information, and security. You will enjoy and understand people better only when you spend time with them. There's a tendency to form a bond with other people when you are with them.

Without people, life is unbearable. Can you imagine being the only one on this earth, or being the only person at the mall? That's why isolation is still the most effective punishment for crimes today.

Redirect Your Time

Just because you don't have more than 24 hours a day doesn't mean you can't get everything done. How much time you have is not as significant as the quality of your time. The more valuable you make your time, the more you will get out of it.

People who make effective use of their time "think in terms of objectives rather than activities; they make most decisions quickly; they speak and write concisely; they avoid procrastination; they treat their time as the precious and limited resource that it is."[1]

How can you get the most done? Simple, redirect your time. With your *Inventory of Twenty-Four Hours*, you can see what you are spending time on. When you are watching a movie on TV, for example, you can use commercial breaks to get your clothes ready for the next day. During your commute to and from work, you could read or listen to an inspiring book (audio versions of many books are readily available). During your break, you can budget for next month. Playtime and personal development can be combined.

Delegating some responsibilities to others is also effective. Instead of doing everything alone, get help. Instead of cooking every day, you can go to a restaurant when you are tired. You can employ a moving service instead of trying to break your back relocating. Sure, all this costs money, but as you overcome racism, you will make your time more valuable. You will have more money to make your life easier.

Whatever can be learned, can be controlled.

MAKE YOUR HABITS WORK FOR YOU

Trina broke up with Walker because he beat her whenever he got angry. Three abusive relationships later, she's now involved with William who beats her whenever he gets drunk.

Although there were no assigned seats, everyone continued to sit in the same spot throughout the semester.

Martha is eighty pounds overweight and still bloating. She has tried just about every weight loss program without success. Whenever she can't get her way, she becomes depressed and goes on an eating spree.

The Merriam-Webster Dictionary defines habit as "a behavior pattern acquired by frequent repetition." You go to the same places, use the same products, go from one abusive relationship to another, continue to overeat, and sometimes act self-destructive because of habits.

Your personality is characterized by your habits—what you do, how you act, what you say, and more. These habits ultimately determine your successes or failures in life. "Habits are powerful factors in our lives," Stephen Covey wrote in *7 Habits of Highly Effective People*. "Because they are consistent, often unconscious patterns, they constantly, daily, express our character and produce our effectiveness . . . or ineffectiveness."[1]

Your habits determine how people treat you. When people become aware of your habits, they regulate their habits to either coincide with or repel yours. If you are in the habit of being reliable, for example, people become convinced that you are dependable. Your supervisor may not hesitate to give you a promotion. Your parents will not worry when they leave you to house-sit while they are away on vacation. People will even take risks with you, because they know that you will not let them down.

Whereas, if you have the habit of taking a few items from work that don't belong to you (so-called white collar crime—office supplies, for example), people start to lock up when you are around.

Habits also determine how you treat other people. When you have the habit of stereotyping all whites as racists, you will feel a courteous white person is patronizing you. When a white person is inconsiderate, you will feel he/she is acting that way because you are black.

Habit Is What You Let It Be

There is a tendency to think of habit as something negative or annoying. People often refer to habits of nail biting, thumb sucking, alcohol or drug dependency, and other acts that do not bring any apparent worthwhile benefits.

Habits are also positive. In fact, habits are the best mechanisms you have operating for you. Habits can help you develop beneficial characteristics that make life fulfilling; they can multiply your productiveness. Habits can also help you completely reverse the typical stereotyped notion held about black people.

Developing good habits is much easier than developing bad ones. Why? Because when you develop good habits, you get positive results. You become happy with yourself and others become happy with you. Your desire and anticipation increase because each day seems to get better. You look forward to waking up every morning.

On the contrary, when you develop bad habits, you are often miserable. You cannot control yourself because habits control you. You may want to kick the bad habits but don't have the power to do so. Eventually, you end up feeling like a loser. Your bad habits annoy others. Your unhappiness with yourself causes you to hurt other people—emotionally and/or physically. Consequently, racism is aggravated.

Are bad habits worth hurting yourself and others over? You can replace negative habits with worthwhile ones. In this chapter, I'll show you easy ways to rid yourself of bad habits by developing and maintaining good habits.

The Two Keys That Influence Habits

Any kind of habit, good or bad, is formed and influenced by basically reward and repetition. Reward is the most important factor in forming a habit; it motivates you to act. The expectation of a reward encourages you to repeat an act until the act becomes a habit.

Ivan Pavlov, a Russian physiologist, did extensive *conditioning* experiments with animals, especially dogs. During the experiment, Pavlov would ring a bell just before placing food in front of some dogs. After repeating the experiment several times, the dogs developed the habit of salivating whenever they heard the bell, even if there was no food.[2] They had learned to associate the sound of the bell with food. The bell caused the dogs to expect a reward—food—so they drooled. The repetition of the experiment made the dogs' habit—drooling to the sound of the bell—spontaneous.

When you are first exposed to drugs, you may not feel any special desire to use them, like the sound of the bell did not have any particular meaning to the dogs in Pavlov's experiments, at first. But after repeatedly using drugs, you fall victim to a deceptive *conditioning* and drugs take on a whole new meaning—the reward of escaping reality. This deceptive reward leads to repetition. And repetition forms habit. Consequently, you may be willing to do whatever it takes just to get high.

How to Develop and Control Habits

If you can walk, drive a car, ride a bicycle, do the electric slide, or even think, you are already qualified to learn how to develop and manipulate habits to help you overcome racism.

Here are some simple strategies to make developing any habit an easy process:

Don't Try to Quit a Bad Habit, Substitute It with a Worthwhile Habit

Trying to quit a negative, deceptive habit is one of the most difficult tasks. Quitting a bad habit requires too much effort. Once your mind and body become attuned to a particular habit, quitting becomes almost impossible. If you were trying to quit smoking, for example, fighting the urge to smoke after a meal will not help you. You may be successful for a few minutes, but the urge to smoke will most likely win. You want to know why? Because while you are thinking: "I will not have a cigarette," your mind is recognizing and picking up the word "cigarette." Since your mind can relate to cigarette only as "got to have it," your mind alerts your physiological addiction. You start to come up with reasons why you should have just one more cigarette before finally quitting.

Quitting a bad habit is virtually impossible; thus, the saying: "A leopard doesn't change its spots," is popular. "Making an effort to refrain from the bad habit," the late Dr. Knight Dunlap discovered, "actually reinforced the habit."[3]

On the other hand, when you redirect your effort to acquire a good habit, your psychological and physiological responses conform to the new habit. Let's go back to the example of the smoking habit. If you had determined that you often crave a cigarette after a meal, during a break, or when you are stressed, changing your routine at these critical times can help you overcome your urge to smoke.

If you hang out in the break room after a meal, try going for a walk instead. If you sit idle just before smoking, try engaging in a physically or mentally stimulating activity—aerobics, or a crossword puzzle, for example. The key is to get involved with an interesting activity. The objective is to delay your mind and eventually your body from getting into the smoking mode. As you become involved with another activity, you will discover that you think less about smoking. Eventually, your new habit will become a substitute for the smoking habit.

Overcoming any bad habit requires basically similar techniques. The strategies you apply to overcoming a smoking habit can be tailored to overcoming racism. You can substitute habits that aggravate racial stereotypes with habits that alleviate racism.

Decide Which Habits You Want to Develop

Knowing what you want to accomplish will simplify the habit formation process. If you want to develop a particular habit, learn all you can about that habit. Observe people who possess the habit you want to develop. Read articles or books on the particular habit. Anything that can help you relate to the habit will make developing the habit easier.

If you decided that you wanted to develop the habit of playing football like a pro, for example, listening to and taking advice from your coach, reading football magazines, watching football games and studying the players' movements will help you improve your playing.

Be Attentive When Forming Habits

Since habit is formed by repetition, the quality of the repetition determines the quality of the habit. Performing the repetition of a habit correctly during the developmental stage, ensures that you develop a strong and positive habit. Learn a habit accurately and you will always perform it right.

The first couple of repetitions require the most effort. Once you become accustomed to a habit, you will require less attention to perform the habit. Can you remember when you were learning to drive a car? You probably had to concentrate just to stay in your lane. You had to keep your head straight to keep going straight. Taking your eyes off the road for a second to read traffic signs, may have been difficult. Remember how the car seemed to followed the direction of your eyes? But with adequate coaching from your driving instructor, and attentive repetition, you learned to drive and read traffic signs simultaneously.

Be Regular

Can you run five miles without stopping to take a break? You probably can do so if you are in perfect shape and jog regularly. If you do not perform a task regularly, you will soon become "rusty." Have you noticed how hard it is to get back in shape when you slack off? Even professional athletes get out of shape if they don't keep up their training.

During the habit formation, regularity is crucial. The more you perform a task, the easier performing the task becomes. Have you noticed perfect moves in a professional basketball game? Are you mesmerized by the contestants in the figure skating Olympics? The athletes' performances are so graceful. The professional athletes perform with ease because of regular practice.

Don't Give in to Obstacles

You encounter obstacles each day of your life. The traffic causes you to be late for your appointment, the snow storm slows you down, you lock your keys in the car, the day-care calls you to pick up your little one who is burning with fever. But how often do you let these obstacles hinder your progress? You work around them. You try to get to work despite the storm. You leave home early to beat the traffic. When you come to a detour, you don't stop and cry just because the street is being repaired, you simply follow the alternate route.

There are times when you are developing a new, positive habit, that you will become too discouraged to continue. But never give in to obstacles. Consider the reward of possessing the habit you are trying to develop. Slow down when you encounter obstacles, if you have to. Take a little break if necessary, but don't give up. Developing any positive habit is worth the effort. Moreover, in a matter of time, your habit will become automatic.

Be Gradual

Did your kindergarten teacher teach you algebra? Most likely not, unless you were a prodigy. In the beginning of your school days, your teacher started teaching you how to count, then simple addition, subtraction, multiplication, and more. What would have happened if your teacher had tried to teach you algebra in the first grade? You probably would have become frustrated.

Your ability varies from task to task. Use your discretion; don't try to push yourself too hard. Start gradually; give your mind and body time to adapt to the habit you are developing. In time, you will be able to do anything, one step at a time.

Crucial Habits

People are capable of developing virtually countless number of habits. But there are some habits that are worth developing because they form the basis of every other habit. Here they are:

The Habit of Starting

You can have the most fascinating dreams, or talk about all the desires you will accomplish, but unless you actually make the effort to succeed, you don't get anywhere.

Taking that first step can be difficult because of so many expectations and concerns. You may procrastinate simply because you can't get that "push" to start.

The best way to develop the habit of starting is to count down. Before you start a habit, say to yourself: "I will start at the count of zero." Clear your mind and commence your count down. When you reach zero, start!

Don't plan every move, especially not at the beginning. Just start with an open mind. Once you get started, apply the methods I discussed earlier for developing habits.

The Habit of Staying Focused

There will always be distractions. Have you noticed how an unexpected event always seems to disrupt you every time you try to accomplish something? Why? Because life is full of many variables. Since everything is constantly changing, you should guard against distraction.

If you are on your way to work, window-shopping would be impractical. If you stop at every store, you could end up being late for work. Moreover, you could forget about work.

Once you have decided what you want to accomplish, stick with it. You can modify your actions periodically as required by prevailing circumstances, but be especially careful not to head off in a completely different direction. If you were in medical school to become an orthopedist, for example, you could decide to switch to cosmetic surgery because the demand is greater and the pay is excellent. But leaving medical school for the Ocean Science Institute because oceanographers are getting an increase in pay may be ludicrous.

There are times when a complete change is necessary, but before you make any drastic move, do your homework. Ascertain that changing focus is in your best interest. Consider both the immediate and long term advantages.

The Habit of Excellence

While racism is a major problem in the United States, excellence is the number one obsession. The competition in all walks of life is intense. People want to look their best and they want superior products and services. You want the most reliable car you can afford. When you are hungry, you go to visit the restaurant that has the most delicious food.

There is one amazing quality about excellence: the opportunity to excel is constantly available to everyone. Every second of your life, you have an opportunity to do a task better. When you are the best in your chosen profession, no one can make you feel worthless.

Excellence is not a one-shot deal; it has to be developed. Seek to excel in everything you do. Strive to improve yourself as much as you can. According to Aristotle, "We are what we repeatedly do. Excellence, then, is not an act, but a habit."

When you are developing the habit of excellence, pretend you are in the spotlight, and your audience is curiously watching every move you make. When you act extraordinarily they will applaud. In reality, your life is really before an audience, especially when you become rich and famous. Don't act in any manner that will reinforce racial stereotype. Instead, overcome racism by being the best in all that you do.

The Habit of Correction

Correction is a never ending process. When you are thirsty, you drink. When it gets dark, turning on the lights is a correction. When your body temperature rises, you sweat. Even dear Mother Nature makes corrections—sometimes when the weather is too hot, she sends rain.

Making little corrections as often as necessary is easier and more practical than making one large correction. Let's take hunger, for example; eating is a form of correction whenever you are hungry. But, could you eat about $168,000 worth of food at one sitting so that you never feel hungry again? That's if you eat-up $50 a week, and live an average of 70 years.

Once developed, the habit of correction becomes like a missile in flight. The missile makes little corrections as often as necessary to remain on course. Eventually, the missile reaches its target.

The Habit of Being Organized

Developing the habit of being organized has tremendous advantages. Being organized saves you time because whatever you need is readily accessible. Instead of getting frustrated trying to find a document, for example, you would know exactly where to look.

To cultivate the habit of being organized, start by grouping similar items together. If you are at home, for example, put the keys in one spot, put all your important papers in one drawer, put the tools in one area.

You will never run out of opportunities to be organized. Items can always be organized and reorganized. For example, if you kept all your important papers in one drawer, you could put all the credit card receipts in one envelope, the grocery receipts in another envelope. The birth certificates could be in another, and so on.

If you need your birth certificate, you will know exactly where to find it instead of scrambling frantically through stacks of other papers. If there was an emergency and you needed to send someone to pick up a particular document, he/she wouldn't have difficulty finding what you needed.

Some people tend to associate being organized with professionalism. When they enter your home or office and see your possessions neatly organized, they immediately start to think that you are an organized person. And they may even compliment you. Most of all, you will not have to come up with some lame excuse like: "Please excuse the mess, I was in such a hurry."

Unless you try a new approach, you will continue getting the same results when you do the same things.

MOTIVATION: DESIRE WORKS MIRACLES

I watched little Hanna Mae learn to walk. Sometimes, she wanted to come to me. Other times, she was interested only in getting to the coffee table to knock something off it. But many times, Hanna Mae seemed bored crawling around; she simply wanted to walk like everyone else. So, she kept trying to take those first few steps. At the start, Hanna Mae would lose her balance, but she didn't give up. She would grab onto my pants, her mother's dress, or the furniture for support. Hanna Mae walked better with each try. Eventually, she didn't need any support. Today, my little daughter is quite a walker, and a runner too.

Learning to walk is an experience most people can relate to. When you were young, you didn't just sit around waiting for someone to move you, you tried to crawl, and later walk. You risked falling and getting hurt because you wanted to walk. The sore bums, little bruises and racism didn't stop you. When you fell, you got up and tried walking again. You didn't learn to walk overnight; you were patient. Every day, you tried a little harder. And here you are today, walking with ease.

Why were you so determined to walk? Walking definitely made you more mobile. You could walk to the bathroom. You could walk like everyone else. You could follow mama around the house. You wanted to walk and you did it.

The power to succeed is within you. You have proven your ability to succeed in some way or another. You can be successful again, as often as you want. Whatever you want to achieve in life, you can rekindle the urge to succeed.

Motivation is the "inner urge," according to *The Random House Dictionary*, which causes you to act "with a sense of purpose." Motivation is the desire within that causes you to persevere when you want to obtain a goal. Motivation enabled Muhammad Ali, a Kentucky youth who "was often bloodied or knocked on his rear end by more experienced fighters," to become "the greatest" prizefighter.[1] Motivation enabled General Colin Powell, whose parents were immigrants from Jamaica, to advance to become the first African-American Chairman of the Joint Chiefs of Staff—the country's top military advisory group. The list can go on and on.

Whatever you want to accomplish, you will succeed if the desire to do so is strong enough. According to *Psychology*, you are motivated by both internal and external needs.[2] Your desire for sleep causes you to close your eyes. You may do whatever is necessary for your peers to accept you. Your desire to overcome racism causes you to read this book.

Wanting to succeed by itself is not enough; you have to be motivated. Motivation is infectious; it causes people around you to want to help you succeed. When you are motivated to overcome racism, you will do so.

Here are some strategies to keep the fire of motivation burning hot inside you:

Look for the Benefit

You do whatever you do because of some conscious or unconscious benefit. Why do you want equality? Because you want to be treated fairly. Why do you want our streets to be crime-free? For the benefit of safety.

The benefit(s) for each of us may vary. Ask some people the same questions and you will probably get many different answers. Why are you reading this book? Someone may say because the title is interesting, another may say because they want to learn to overcome racism, someone may say because they are bored and need something to do. But no matter what benefits people seek, they are motivated to do what they do.

Sometimes, the benefit is not immediately apparent, but all the same it lies out there somewhere. One day, a little friend, who I'll call Justin, came to talk to me. He was obviously frustrated. "Why is my mama making such a fuss about school?" he complained. "She keeps telling me she wants me to have a better life than her." He paused a little, but continued after he didn't get a response from me, "I hate school and I hate homework. Man, I can hardly wait for summer."

I thought about the situation for a moment; it all made sense. How could little Justin comprehend the benefit of school? He lived at home with his mama. He didn't know how the rent was paid. Justin didn't have to worry about car payments. Would it then be all right for Justin to "goof off" in school because there wasn't any apparent benefit? Certainly not.

"Justin," I responded, "name ten things you want the most."

His little brown eyes beamed up. "I want to go to Disney World, I want a bicycle, I want lots of chocolates and candies, I want . . ." The kid kept on going, even after he had named eleven things he wanted.

"OK, Mr. Justin," I said, "when you do well in school, you'll hopefully be able to buy all the things you want. Best of all, you will be able to do what you enjoy doing. What do you want to be when you grow up?"

"I want to be a mechanic so I can fix my mama's car whenever it breaks down," he replied.

"See," I said, "school can help you become the best mechanic."

The advantages of an education gave Justin a new perspective on school. By searching for possible benefit(s), you will feel the need to excel in whatever you have to do, even if the task seems boring at first.

Set a Deadline

Setting a deadline will enable you to allocate your time and resources effectively. Deadlines keep you focused because you have a definite time frame to work with.

A deadline keeps you motivated by adding some pressure. People generally tend to act under pressure. If you have to be at work by nine o'clock, you will leave home early enough to get to work on time. Without some degree of pressure, procrastination takes control. And nothing gets done.

Stick to your deadlines as closely as possible. Deadlines have some astonishing rewards. You get your project done and end up feeling like a winner. You feel motivated to tackle another task. You become confident when you succeed.

Surround Yourself with Positive People

Being around positive people is rewarding—spiritually, physically, and emotionally. Positive people will help steer you away from trouble. Because of their positive attitudes, they will not want to see you fail.

Positive people are an unlimited source of motivation. Because positive people have loving attitudes, you will be encouraged to strive for excellence. You will not want to do anything to disappoint them. Psychological studies indicate that a group has quite an influence on its members. If the group is positive, the members tend to be positive also.

Positive people are a source of emotional support. When you feel discouraged, they will often reassure you that you can succeed. And you will easily believe them.

Read Inspiring Books

There are books on every subject imaginable—business, sex, housekeeping, racism, medicine, poetry, dancing, you name it. But not every book is of interest to you. In fact, some books even contradict your convictions.

Read inspiring books as often as you can. The time you invest in reading "good" books is rewarding. Inspiring books will motivate you to succeed. Some inspiring books can teach you how to succeed at a specific task. Books can help you avoid expensive mistakes. Through reading, you can quickly learn secrets that other people took years to discover. The knowledge you obtain from reading could save you thousands of dollars, open a door of opportunities, or even help you meet that special someone.

Your local library carries many books that you'll find beneficial. You can borrow these books at little or no charge.

Listen to Your Favorite Music

Music motivates people. You can experiment with the magical effects of music. Try doing a tedious task—aerobics, for example—to your favorite tunes. You will notice how much easier your task seems. Music has a way of making strenuous tasks fun.

A marketing study concluded that music influences people's attitudes. In an experiment, people were shown products with accompanying music. An overwhelming number of people chose the products that were accompanied by "pleasant music."[3]

Finding the music that suites you is easy; just listen without prejudice, and you will find lots of music that makes you experience an indescribable feeling of motivation.

Visit Places of Interest

Places influence people. Take a trip to Hollywood and you'll feel like a star. Go to the airport and you may feel like traveling. Visit Disneyland and you will feel like a kid. Remember the uneasy feeling you get when you go to the hospital? Have you noticed the creepy feeling you get when you are in a cemetery?

Going to places that interest you is a rewarding experience. Whenever you visit places of interest you learn something new. Moreover, you become motivated. When I was growing up, I often stopped by the airport before and after school to admire the planes takeoff and land. On weekends, I would hang around the hangars to talk to pilots. Each time I visited the airport, I learned something new about aviation. Most of all, I became more determined to learn to fly.

If you want to be a basketball star, go to basketball courts, stadiums, domes, anywhere there are basketball games. If you want to be a medical doctor, visit hospitals. If you want to overcome racism, visit places that depict African-American suffering—the Civil Rights Memorial, in Montgomery, Alabama, for example. And you will be motivated to succeed.

Break Your Tasks into Smaller Parts

Overcoming racism may seem like a major undertaking, but if you break up the various steps—building self-confidence, becoming educated, motivated, and more—you will have a better chance of being successful. When you break up your tasks into smaller jobs, you have only one part to concentrate on at a time.

If you wanted to get on top of the roof to repair a leak, could you jump right up like some bionic man/woman? Maybe in Hollywood, but in real life, you will have to climb up. If you decided to use a ladder, climb up one rung at a time, your job would be much easier. Also, you could avoid the frustration of not being able to jump to the top of the roof.

When you look at the "big picture," you are right if you see impossibilities. But try breaking up your tasks, and you will almost immediately see possibilities. You cannot accomplish the "big picture" at a single shot, any more than you can expect to be promoted to the rank of general upon enlisting in the service. But, it's possible to become a private, so is becoming a sergeant, and so on. The better you perform at these "relatively" smaller possibilities, the greater your chance of moving up to the next higher rank.

Here is what Dale Carnegie said about succeeding at parts of your task: "Don't be afraid to give your best to what seemingly are small jobs. Every time you conquer one, it makes you that much stronger. If you do the little jobs well, the big ones will tend to take care of themselves."

Focus on the "Rights" in Your Life

To overcome racism, you must focus on utilizing the positive aspects in your life, rather than on dwelling on the drawbacks of being black. You may not have accomplished too much at the present, but look at all you have going for you. For example, time, habits, access to beneficial information, role models, scholarships, opportunities to be successful, and so much more. So, why should you constantly worry about the store clerk who treats you like a shoplifter? Why lose your nerve over a racial slur? Don't let racism hurt you.

According to Dale Carnegie:

> About ninety percent of the things in our lives are right and about ten percent are wrong. If we want to be happy, all we have to do is to concentrate on the ninety percent that are right and ignore the ten percent that are wrong. If we want to be worried and bitter and have stomach ulcers, all we have to do is to concentrate on the ten percent that are wrong and ignore the ninety percent that are glorious.

When you focus on the "rights" in your life, you are actually focusing on possibilities. If you can perceive opportunities to succeed, you may get tempted to be successful.

Minimize Your Worries

If you want to overcome racism, you have to stop worrying about being black. Worries of any kind are counterproductive. Worries are like thieves that steal your happiness. Worries are even bad for your health; medical studies have long associated worrying with various illnesses.

When you are faced with a new task, there is a tendency to worry about the unknown. You worry about failing. You worry about people staring at you because you are black. You worry that people will think you are stupid. You worry about disappointing others. You worry about getting laid off from work. You worry and worry.

When you worry, your mind comes up with more paranoiac reasons why you should worry. You expect your fears to come true. Consequently, you prepare yourself psychologically and physically for your shortcomings. Inevitably, your worries are ratified. Then you can reassuringly say, "It's because I'm black."

Worrying keeps you entrapped in a vicious circle. When you worry, there is a propensity to use negative experiences from the past to destroy a promising future. A young lady I'll call Ashley always complained about not having anyone to love her for who she was. Well, somehow, Ashley later became involved with an intelligent, dependable, professional and charitable gentleman.

Ashley told me, during a casual conversation one day, that she was afraid of losing her boyfriend. She asked for my advice. I told her to love him and treat him well.

"I'm scared to love him; all the men I've ever loved always end up leaving me; I don't want to be hurt again," Ashley replied.

I asked her why she thought this guy would leave her.

"With my luck? He'll leave me like the other guys did," she replied.

To cut a long story short, Ashley's worries about her boyfriend leaving her started to interfere with their relationship. She started to prepare herself mentally for his leaving, although he didn't give her any reason to. As a result, Ashley started to hate her boyfriend for what she thought he might do to her.

Ashley was punishing her boyfriend for what the other men had done to her. Ashley's boyfriend interpreted her behavior as any self-confident man would; he saw her as a confused person. He eventually broke up with Ashley, not because he had planned to, but because he got tired of the way she treated him.

Whenever you find yourself worrying, break the vicious circle by playing "what if." What if you succeeded? What if everything worked out for the better? What if you overcame racism? Consider the best outcome for your situation. At least, thinking positively or constructively makes you feel much better.

Dance Your Troubles Away

Whenever you feel depressed, sad, worried or just bored, dance. Dancing has a way of making you feel better about yourself; it releases the creativity within you. Dancing makes you happy.

I've always been curious about why the Caribbean Islanders and people living south of the border are so cheerful. Although the standard of living in some of these countries is below those that many of us are used to in the states, the people down there still seem so happy. During one of my dive trips to the Caribbean, I asked an islander what the secret to their happiness is. She answered with a smile, "We dance our troubles away."

You don't have to go to some fancy night club to dance; you can dance at home. Turn the music up; use a headset if you might disturb others. You don't necessarily need a dance partner; you can do fine by yourself. Turn the lights down or close the blinds. Just listen to the music; let it flow through your being. Let your body move. Don't try to imitate anyone's style. Your movements will soon settle into your body's natural rhythm. If you are shy, close your eyes. Don't think; you cannot worry if you are not thinking. Dance and enjoy every minute of it. You will almost immediately start to feel the difference.

"Dancing is the loftiest, the most moving, the most beautiful of the arts, because it is no mere translation or abstraction from life; it is life itself," said Havelock Ellis. You are alive and deserve to experience life; dance all those troubles—racism, especially—away.

Recommended Reading

Peale, Norman Vincent. The Power of Positive Thinking. Englewood Cliffs: Prentice, 1952.

There are only three times: one when it is too early,
one when the time is just right, and one when it is too late.

OVERCOMING RACISM IS EASIER NOW THAN EVER

Overcoming racism has never been easier than now. During slavery, overcoming racism would have been virtually impossible because animosity was super-abundant. If you wait much longer to overcome racism, it may be too late. Discrimination, hate crimes and violence could escalate beyond control.

Now is the time to overcome racism. African-Americans' greatest problem is now most vulnerable because:

Racism Is Exposed

You are now aware of how racism affects your decisions, attitude, and progress. In chapter four of this book, you saw the similarity between discrimination in Africa, Asia, Europe, Middle-East and the United States. Although people around the world base their discrimination on different traits, the effects of discrimination are similar.

Most importantly, you now know that you are not wrong. Racism is wrong. Hating people because of their race is wrong. Prejudging people is wrong. The need to feel superior to others is wrong. Allowing racism to hurt you is wrong.

Also, you now have easy strategies to overcome racism. Many African-Americans have overcome racism to rise to the top of their chosen endeavors. You too can succeed by overcoming racism.

You've Got the Power

Not very long ago, blacks were lynched like animals, worked like machines, used and abused like disposable objects. Blacks' destinies were in the hands of slave masters. African-Americans dreamed and prayed for freedom. They risked their lives to end segregation.

Today, thanks to all who made freedom possible for African-Americans, you can sleep, wake up, work, or do whatever you want, whenever you want. Your destiny is in your hands now. There are laws designed to protect you from physical or verbal abuse, discrimination in employment and housing, and more. Overcoming racism is now entirely up to you.

There Are Opportunities to Advance

How many National Guardsmen will you need to escort you to school? How large a welcoming audience jeering racial slurs at you do you expect at school? How often do you expect to be refused service at a restaurant? Do you anticipate a conductor will insist that you sit only in the back of the bus? Will you be forced to give up your seat to a non-black person? These are only a few contempts that blacks had to contend with before desegregation.

Now, if you want to and are qualified, you can attend the most prestigious school in the country. You can learn with the most scholarly. You can become the best of the best. If you cannot afford to go to college, there are many scholarships and financial aid plans specifically for helping young African-Americans—United Negro College Fund (UNCF) is one of many such programs. President Clinton's voluntary service for college students will enable you to finance your education without getting into debt from student loans.

African-Americans Are Moving up in Social Status

African-Americans are increasingly making progress. The black middle-class is getting bigger, is better educated, and more successful. A study conducted by *The Washington Post* gave the following indications of a growing black middle-class:

- The majority of the Washington area's 650,000 blacks live in its suburbs, not in the District of Columbia.

- Of the area's 300,000 prosperous blacks, almost twice as many live in mostly white neighborhoods as in mostly black ones.

- In the four largest counties—Fairfax and Prince William in Virginia and Montgomery and Prince George's in Maryland, the typical black family makes between $1,100 and $5,200 more a year than does the typical white family elsewhere in the United States.

- The typical Washington area young black—age 25 to 29—has more education than the typical young white elsewhere in the United States. In Montgomery County, the black median is higher by an entire college semester.

- Since 1980, the fastest-growing population of young blacks in absolute numbers in the region's public schools has been in Fairfax and Montgomery counties.[1]

African-Americans Have Major Economic Power

African-Americans now have a large buying power—$263 billion as reported by the 1990 census. Many African-Americans can now afford to buy luxury cars, go on pleasure cruises, eat at the fanciest restaurants, live in middle to upper-class neighborhoods, shop at expensive stores, to name a few.

Many businesses are aware of African-Americans' substantial financial leverage. Businesses' marketing strategies are targeting African-Americans' patronage. You have probably noticed the increased number of black actors and actresses in commercials on national television. National chain stores are also carrying a variety of African-American products—there is even the black Barbie doll, for example.

During segregation, African-Americans used their buying power to help change separatism. Although blacks patronized many businesses—the bus service, restaurants, stores, hotels, and more—they were still mistreated. So when African-Americans started to boycott businesses, the loss of revenues and adverse publicity made businesses reconsider their segregation policies.

The threat of boycott is still effective today. A popular occurrence was in 1993 when the National Football League (NFL), threatened to boycott the Superbowl in Arizona. The state had refused to make the late Dr. Martin Luther King, Jr.'s birthday a holiday. Arizona immediately reconsidered its decision.

African-Americans Have Political Power

Shortly after the Civil War, racists made every effort to keep blacks from achieving political power. Racists tried to discourage African-Americans from voting.

> [Blacks who did vote] were refused jobs, medical treatment, or service in stores. In many instances blacks weren't allowed to vote at all. Armed patrols kept them away from the polling place, or the location of the polling place was kept secret from them.[2]

The political atmosphere has improved for African-Americans. Record number of African-Americans now hold political positions at federal, state, and local levels. Many prominent US cities—Washington, DC, New York, Atlanta, New Orleans, to name only a few—have/had black mayors. African-Americans are also in the senate—Carol Moseley Braun, for example, was the first African-American woman elected to the United States Senate in 1992.

People Are More Tolerant

Surveys have shown that whites are now more tolerant of blacks in general. From observation around the country, there are many whites and non-blacks who have black supervisors. There are also many integrated neighborhoods.

African-Americans are more versatile. There are blacks in the aerospace industry—Mae C. Jemison, a scholarly young woman and also the country's first African-American female astronaut. Toni Morrison was the first African-American woman to receive the Nobel Prize for literature. There are professional African-American golfers, figure skaters, hockey players, to name only a few.

As whites and other ethnic groups are increasingly exposed to African-Americans' versatility, they will have the opportunity to see that blacks are real people who are capable of success; hence, old racial stereotypes will be alleviated.

Some businesses and organizations sponsor racial sensitivity seminars to improve cooperation between employees and customers. Schools around the country are including African-American studies in their curriculum.

People Are Coming Together to Alleviate Violence

Many African-American neighborhoods are war zones. Blacks are killing blacks, exploiting and destroying all chances of success for other blacks. African-Americans want positive change. At least 1.5 million people demonstrated their desire for change when they participated in the Million Man March in Washington, DC, on October 16, 1995.[3]

Neighborhood residents are taking active measures—neighborhood watch, for example—to take their streets back from violence. People are tired of the effects of racism—crimes, drugs, violence, to name a few. Residents want their neighborhoods to be safe; therefore, they will welcome any promising solution—overcoming racism, for example.

Every end is only a beginning.

THE END

You have just about come to the end of this book, but the beginning of a new and exciting life. You are capable of turning all your dreams into realities.

Don't place this book on the shelf and forget about it. Keep it handy. Read it; highlight quotes and sentences that interest you. Go to the library and read the suggested books at the end of some chapters.

You Are Capable

Inside of you are capabilities. You have the ability to succeed at any endeavor. Unless you become aware of your capabilities, utilize them, allow them to serve you right, and develop them to their highest level of perfection, they will lie dormant and nothing will happen. You have a real gift within, unwrap and discover it.

Dream Nation

What if the majority of the black population came to recognize their capabilities? What if self-hatred turn into self-respect? What if all black men were like fathers to all black children? What if all black women were like mothers to all black children? What if blacks were united? What if we were all trying to overcome racism? What if the projects became like middle-class neighborhoods? What if all blacks were proud of their color?

If you feel the "what ifs" are dreams, you are right. Remember, the late Dr. Martin Luther King, Jr. and many other people dreamed that someday blacks would be free. Today, we are free. Our destinies lie in our hands.

Dreams do come true, but they don't happen by themselves. People have to turn dreams into realities. The African-American dream of desegregation, for example, didn't materialize easily. For the freedom and desegregation we enjoy today, people defied the unjust laws, protested, marched, struggled, sang and prayed. Many blacks and even whites who were interested in our cause were interrogated, prosecuted, and sometimes murdered.

Fortunately, you don't have to go to the extremes to realize your dreams. Race relations are not perfect, but they are now much better than they were because we are all, as a nation, beginning to discuss the problem openly. You as an individual must improve the racial situation by overcoming racism every time you encounter it.

We Can

We can become the best in any occupation. We can learn to love ourselves. We can learn to love each other like brothers and sisters. We can act like parents to all black children; we can inspire them and keep them safe.

We can come together to lend a helping hand to a fellow black. We can offer each other a shoulder to lean on. Black men can treat black women with respect and unconditional love; black women can treat black men similarly.

We can make being black an honor, something to be proud of. We can take advantage of educational opportunities. We can make people long to have us as neighbors, because they will know that "African-Americans are caring neighbors." People can want us to be members of their organization because "African-Americans are hardworking, motivated individuals who can get the job done." People will want us as friends, not because we are black, but because "blacks are wonderful friends indeed."

We can reconstruct the projects, socially, physically, and emotionally. Projects can become like middle-class neighborhoods for those who cannot afford to flee to the suburbs. Families can be supportive of each other.

We can, we can, and we can. Nevertheless, all these changes won't happen overnight; neither will they happen by themselves. We have to make the changes because we can.

The civil rights leaders can only do so much. The politicians are busy trying to get reelected. The middle-class is trying to move up into the upper-class. The lower-class is busy trying to move up or keep up with the changing economy. However, together, we can do the apparently impossible.

Overcoming racism is a *race* effort. A race which you are automatically a part of. A race with too much stigma attached. You can no more run away from being black than you can run away from your shadow. If we become united and work together, we can change our lives for the better, forever.

Don't look to others to make the change for you; they may be looking to you. With each of us doing our part—becoming the best that we possibly can be—blacks can soon come to realize respect, equality, excellence, and much more.

We Are Survivors

African-Americans endured humiliation, torture, segregation, hatred, and murder, yet, the black race is still surviving. We truly are children of the dream if all the animosity didn't annihilate us. Overcoming racism by developing ourselves to be creative individuals, becoming happy with ourselves, and being able to enjoy life ought to be the goals we survivors seek now.

The Choice Is Yours

While I was growing up, my dad often said: "Son, life is what you make of it." I would like to substitute the word "future" for "life." *My dear brothers and sisters, the future is what we make of it.*

In this capitalist world, excellence still dominates prejudice and skin color. Excellence is achievable. In order to overcome racism, you must excel in whatever endeavor you choose. You owe it to the past, because you cannot betray those who struggled, and even gave up their lives, for the freedom you enjoy today. You owe it to the present, because without striving for excellence, you are doomed to experience the past. You owe it to the future, because you have to pave the way for the younger generation.

You can overcome racism, but you have to choose to do so. God bless.

The Beginning

Appendix

There are thousands of resources—organizations, books, seminars, programs, to name only a few—available to help you overcome racism. The author has compiled a list of some valuable resources.

Organizations

Black Awareness in Television
13217 Livernois
Detroit, MI 48238-3162
(313) 931-3427

Black Awareness in Television trains people in the media and conducts surveys. This organization also produces African-American media programs for television, video, theater, and radio.

Congress of Racial Equality (CORE)
1457 Flatbush Ave.
Brooklyn, NY 11210
(718) 434-3580

CORE is a human rights organization that promotes equality for people of all racial or ethnic origins.

Council for a Black Economic Agenda (CBEA)
1367 Connecticut Ave. NW
Washington, DC 20036
(202) 331-1103

The Council for a Black Economic Agenda encourages African-Americans to become successful entrepreneurs; thereby, alleviating many blacks' dependencies on federal programs.

National Association for the Advancement of Colored People (NAACP)
4805 Mt. Hope Drive
Baltimore, MD 21215
(301) 358-8900

NAACP's objective is to end racism in education, voting, employment, housing, and society as a whole.

United Negro College Fund (UNCF)
500 E. 62nd St.
New York, NY 10021
(212) 326-1118

UNCF is a fundraising agency for fully accredited, historically black private colleges, universities, graduate, and professional schools. The UNCF also awards scholarships to qualified minority students.

Many organizations publish a newsletter or magazine. Call or write them for more information. Because the listing was compiled upon publication of this book, some of the addresses and/or phone numbers may have changed. However, you can get an updated address or phone number from the *Black Americans Information Directory*, a reference published by Gale. Or see a librarian at the reference desk in your local library.

Books

Jones, Rochelle. <u>The Big Switch: New Careers, New Lives, After 35</u>. New York: McGraw-Hill, 1980.

The author gives valuable self-help strategies for anyone, younger than or older than 35 years, who is considering a career change.

Morin, William, and James Cabrera. <u>Parting Company: How to Survive the Loss of a Job and Find Another Successfully</u>. New York: Harcourt, 1982.

This book offers helpful advice on coping with unemployment, looking for another job, and marketing yourself.

Lipman, Burton. <u>The Professional Job Search Program: How to Market Yourself</u>. New York: Wiley, 1983.

Lipman offers suggestions on resume preparation, finding possible job openings, applying for positions, conducting oneself during an interview, and much more.

Goldstein, Jerome. <u>In Business for Yourself</u>. New York: Scribner's, 1982.

Goldstein uses case studies to show the fulfillment of successfully owning and operating a small business.

These books are available at your local bookstore. Or you can get them from your local library. If the library doesn't have copies, you can order them through the interlibrary loan.

Glossary

Affirmative Action Programs Policies that mandate organizations to consider race, sex, and ethnic origin in decision making. (45)

Aid to Families with Dependent Children (AFDC) A federal program that assists single low-income parent with children. (69)

Aircraft Owners and Pilots Association (AOPA) An organization for pilots and aircraft owners, which offers advice on aviation matters, legal representation, online services, discounted aeronautic charts, and a lot more, to its members. (91)

Americo-Liberians A group of people, also called Conquers, whose descendants returned to Africa after slavery was aboloshed. (28)

Association An organization whose members have a common objective. (90-92)

Basic needs Necessities—food, clothing and shelter—which must be satisfied in order to sustain life. (71)

Birthright A privilege that one is entitled to. (44)

Caste A social position inherited by a group of people. (26)

Chinese Exclusion Act A law passed by congress in 1882 to ban Chinese from coming to the United States for ten years. (26)

Chipping Using a specially designed tool to break off rust in small pieces from a ship. (81)

Civil rights leaders People—the late Dr. Martin Luther King, Jr., for example—who promote or ensure that other people's nonpolitical rights as citizens are not violated. (5)

Comfort zone A situation that one is used to. (54)

Conditioning A response that becomes habitual due to a stimulus. For example, someone locking his/her car door whenever a black man is in the vicinity. (119-20)

Deck A platform resembling a floor. Also, a ship excluding the engine room. (81)

Deckhand A sailor who performs manual labor. (81)

Desegregation To abolish segregation by including people of all races and ethnicity without restriction. (148)

Discrimination To act in favor of or against someone because of prejudice. (23)

Downsizing Decreasing the size of an organization by terminating some positions. (96-97)

Entrepreneur Someone who organizes, promotes, and manages a business. (47)

Facial feedback hypothesis An assumption that a person's facial expression influences his/her mood. (73)

Fight-or-flight reaction The body's response to face or avoid an adverse situation. (29)

Genetics The science of the origin and development of something. (16)

Glass ceiling A term used to describe a restriction that is not obvious. (66)

Habit A pattern of behavior resulting from frequent repetitions. (117-27)

Holocaust A massive destruction, usually by fire. For example, the Nazis destroyed over six million Jews. (27)

Hotline A phone line open for immediate response. (92)

Hypnosis A state in which someone voluntarily complies with another person's suggestions. (38)

Indentured Servants Immigrants who worked as slaves for a predetermined number of years in exchange for transportation to the United States. (18)

Integration See desegregation.

Intelligent Quotient (IQ) Test An examination designed to measure one's ability to learn and apply knowledge. (11-12)

Interlibrary loan A process whereby libraries borrow material from other libraries for patrons. (90)

Internet A computer system whereby users can interact with other computer users. (55)

Jim Crow law Segregation laws that prevailed in the South around the nineteenth and twentieth centuries. (29)

Kerner Commission See National Advisory Commission on Civil Disorders.

Know-Nothings A hate group whose members were supposed to declare that they knew nothing whenever they were questioned about their activities. (24)

Magna cum laude A person graduating with a grade point average (GPA) of 3.5 or better. (2)

Mate A deck officer, other than a captain, in the merchant marines. (81)

Motivation A desire to obtain a particular goal. (129-38)

National Advisory Commission on Civil Disorders A group of people appointed by President Lyndon Johnson to study the causes of black riots. The Commission, which was later called the Kerner Commission, after its chairman, Otto Kerner, reported that unemployment, police brutality, unfair housing, media-biased presentation, among many other contemptuous activities, prompted blacks to revolt. (38)

Networking The art of using contacts to keep abreast of changes, and take advantage of opportunities in the professional environment. (101)

Obstacle Anything that prevents someone from accomplishing a goal. (123)

Overboard The act of throwing a person or thing over the railing of a ship and into the sea. Also, falling off a ship. (19)

Patronize Supporting someone by buying his/her product(s) and/or service(s). (47)

Perception The interpretation of people and things within the environment. (36)

Pink slip A job termination notice. (96)

Polygraph A device used to detect when a person is telling a lie. (75)

Prejudice Forming a negative opinion of someone or something without known facts. (40)

Quotas Assigning a proportionate number of openings for a particular group of people. (98)

Ratings A system of determining the popularity of a program, for example, by measuring the number of audience. (34)

Reservation Land issued by the federal government to Native Americans for inhabitation. (25)

Rhinoplasty A plastic surgery procedure for reshaping the nose. (4)

Seaman A laborer with general deck duties—painting, chipping, cleaning, steering—on a merchant ship. (64-65)

Segregation Separating people by race or ethnicity, in public facilities, housing, schools, neighborhoods, and more. (29)

Ship's hold A deep opening in the bottom of a ship, often use to store cargo. (19)

Statistics An orderly arrangement of numeric data from collected facts. (3)

Stigma A mark of disgrace. (5)

Surveillance The act of carefully watching. (10)

Trait A distinguishing characteristic. (10)

Zionism A movement marked by Jews returning to Palestine. (27)

Sources

Chapter 1

1. Galifianakis, Nick. "Homocides: Who's at Risk." <u>USA Today</u> 2 Feb. 1995: 5A. The statistics are contained in the article "Teens in the Cross Fire: `Worst Is Yet to Come'."

2. Adler, Jerry. "Murder." <u>Newsweek</u> 15 Aug. 1994: 26. Statistics are taken from "Who Kills Whom." The source of the statistics is: J. A. Fox and G. Pierce, National Crime Analysis Program, Northeastern University.

3. Edmonds, Patricia. "Teens in the Cross Fire: `Worst Is Yet to Come'." <u>USA Today</u> 2 Feb. 1995: 5A. Edmonds uses elaborate examples and statistics to discuss teenagers and African-American homocides.

4. Mizell, Linda. <u>Think About Racism</u>. New York: Walker, 1992, 160.

5. Edmonds, Patricia. "Bottom Line of Poverty: Study Says It Costs Billions." <u>USA Today</u> 16 Nov. 1994: 3A.

6. Cohan, Paul. "Between a Rock and a Hard Place." <u>American City & County</u> June 1993: 58. The graph on page 58 contains yearly cost per offender in state and federal prisons, local jails and detention centers. Source: The National Committee on Community Corrections.

7. Mizell, Linda. <u>Think About Racism</u>. New York: Walker, 1992, 161.

Chapter 2

1. Taylor, Marian W. <u>Madam C. J. Walker</u>. New York: Chelsea, 1994, 68.

2. Randolph, Laura B. "Oprah Opens Up About Her Weight, Her Wedding and Why She withheld the Book." <u>Ebony</u> Oct. 1993: 131.

3. Begley, Sharon. "Three Is Not Enough." <u>Newsweek</u> 13 Feb. 1995: 68-69.

4. The Associated Press. "` Bell Curve' Theories Wrong, Scholars Says." <u>The Times-Picayune</u> 13 Dec. 1994: A8.

5. Ehrlich, Paul R., and S. Shirley Feldman. <u>The Race Bomb</u>. New York: Quadrangle, 1977, 49-57.

6. Rubin, Zick, and Elton B. McNeil. <u>Psychology</u>. 4th ed. New York: Harper, 1985, 116.

Chapter 3

1. Rubin, Zick, and Elton B. McNeil. <u>Psychology</u>. 4th ed. New York: Harper, 1985, 226.

Chapter 4

1. Thompson, Sharon Elaine. <u>Hate Groups</u>. San Diego: Lucent, 1994, 15.

2. Pascoe, Elaine. <u>Racial Prejudice</u>. New York: Franklin, 1985, 61.

3. Majumdar, D. N. <u>Races and Cultures of India</u>. Bombay: Asia, 1961, 331-32.

4. Rubin, Zick, and Elton B. McNeil. <u>Psychology</u>. 4th ed. New York: Harper, 1985, 359-60.

Chapter 5

1. Cosby, Camille O. <u>Television's Imageable Influences</u>. Lanham: University, 1994, 2.

2. Maltz, Maxwell. <u>Psycho-Cybernetics</u>. New York: Pocket, 1960, 53-54.

3. Walker, Kenneth. "The Nightly News Blues. " <u>Essence</u> Jan. 1993: 104.

4. Johnson, Robert E. "Camille Cosby's Book Explores Negative Images of Blacks In Media." <u>Jet</u> 27 Feb. 1995: 61.

Chapter 8

1. Bernotas, Bob. <u>Spike Lee Filmmaker</u>. Hillside: Enslow, 1993, 27.

2. Ritchie, Barbara. <u>The Riot Report</u>. New York: Viking, 1969, 150.

Chapter 9

1. Carnegie, Dale. <u>Five Minute Biographies</u>. New York: Greenberg, 1937, 143-44.

2. Rubin, Zick, and Elton B. McNeil <u>Psychology</u>. 4th ed. New York: Harper, 1985, 35-47.

3. Carnegie, Dale. <u>How to Win Friends and Influence People</u>. Rev. ed. New York: Simon, 1981, 130.

4. Rubin, Zick, and Elton B. McNeil. <u>Psychology</u>. 4th ed. New York: Harper, 1985, 313.

5. Carnegie, Dale. <u>How to Win Friends and Influence People</u>. Rev. ed. New York: Simon, 1981, 93-94.

Chapter 10

1. H. Norman Wright. How to Get Along with Almost Anyone. Dallas: Word, 1989, 130.

2. McGarvey, Robert. "How to Handle Mean People." Reader's Digest May 1994: 121.

Chapter 12

1. Levington, Marc. "Thanks. You're Fired." Newsweek 23 May 1994: 48.

2. Saltzman, Amy, Mary Lord, and Edward C. Baig. "Voices from the Front." U.S. News and World Report 13 Jan. 1992: 49.

3. The World Almanac and Book of Facts. Mahwah: Funck, 209.

4. Whetstone, Muriel L. "The Story Behind the Explosive Statistics: Why Blacks Are Losing Ground in the Workforce." Ebony Dec. 1993: 104.

5. Mizell, Linda. Think About Racism. New York: Walker, 1992, 156.

6. Whetstone, Muriel L. "The Story Behind the Explosive Statistics: Why Blacks Are Losing Ground in the Workforce." Ebony Dec. 1993: 106

7. Sims, Claudette E. Don't Weep for Me. Houston: Impressions, 1989, 4.

8. Digest of Education Statistics. Washington, DC: U.S. Department of Education, 1992, 385.

Chapter 13

1. Bliss, Edwin C. <u>Getting Things Done</u>. New York: Charles, 1976, 2.

Chapter 14

1. Covey, Stephen. <u>7 Habits of Highly Effective People</u>. New York: Simon, 1989, 46.

2. Dunlap, Knight. <u>Habits: Their Making and Unmaking</u>. New York: Liveright, 1949, 60-62.

3. Maltz, Maxwell. <u>Psycho-Cybernetics</u>. New York: Pocket, 1960, 60.

Chapter 15

1. Macht, Norman. <u>Muhammed Ali</u>. New York: Chelsea, 1994, 18.

2. Rubin, Zick, and Elton B. McNeil. <u>Psychology</u>. 4th ed. New York: Harper, 1985, 296.

3. Rubin, Zick, and Elton B. McNeil. <u>Psychology</u>. 4th ed. New York: Harper, 1985, 457.

Chapter 16

1. <u>Racism in America</u>. San Diego: Greenhaven, 1991, 96.

2. Mizell, Linda. <u>Think About Racism</u>. New York: Walker, 1992, 69.

3. Elie, Lolis Eric. "Marching Men Find Strength in Numbers." <u>The Times-Picayune</u> 17 Oct. 1995: A1. Officers of the National Park Service reported an estimate of 400,000 participants. But, organizers of the march claimed that 1.5 million people were present.

Index

Ability, 124
Affirmative Action, 3, 45
African-Americans, 3-5, 9,
    45, 56, 59, 75
    advancement, 144
    businesses, 47
    economic power, 144
    political power, 145
    unemployment, 44, 48, 66
Africans, 10, 17, 18
Aid to Families with
    Dependent Children
    (AFDC), 69
Aircraft Owners and Pilots
    Association (AOPA),
    91-92
Ali, Muhammad, 130
Americo-Liberians, 28
Anti-Chinese movement, 26
Anti-discrimination laws, 45
Arabs, 27, 107
Aristotle, 126
Asians, 10, 26, 87, 98
Associations, 90-92
Attention
    in habit formation, 122
Attitude, 48, 59, 70

Basic needs, 71
Berenson, Bernard, 108
Black, 5, 13, 45
    children, 3, 21, 148
    men, 3, 20, 148
    middle-class, 143

women, 20, 148

Blaming, 43-44
Body types, 10
Books, inspirational, 112, 133
Bosnia, 27
Bradley, Ed, 39
Braun, Carol Moseley, 145
Break, 114, 123

Capabilities, 46, 147
Carnegie, Dale, 70, 72,
    78, 135
Caste, 26-27
Catholics, 25
Caucasians, 24
Change, life, 52
Charts, aeronautical, 92
Chinese, 26, 46
Chinese Exclusion Act, 26
Chipping rust, 81
Civil rights
    leaders, 5, 45, 149
    memorial, 134
Civil War, 9, 145
Comfort zone, 54
Companionship, 115
Compliment, 76-77
    frivolous, 76
Conditioning, 119-120
Consumers, 97
Contingencies, 83
Control, 48
    negative People, 81

Index

Habit, 117-27
  control, 118
  formation, 121-22
  quitting, 120
  regularity, 122-23
Hamas, 28
Hanna Mae, 51, 129
Happy, 47, 71, 72, 119
Hate, 46, 74, 137
  crimes, 19, 27, 141
  groups, 24, 26
Hatred, 24, 28, 71, 150
Hazlitt, William, 106
Heredity, 15
Hispanic, 10, 87, 98, 107
Hitler, Adolf, 31
Holocaust, 27
Honesty, 75
Hotline, 92
Hunger, satisfying, 126
Hypnotist, 37

Immigrants,
  Asian, 26
  Catholic, 25
Incarcerate, 5, 7
Indenture servants, 18, 19
Inflation, 67, 108
Information, 87-92
  confidential, 89
Instinct for survival, 31
Integration, 11
Intelligence agents, 89
Intelligent Quotient (IQ) Test,
  11-12
Interlibrary loan, 90

Intermarriage, 27, 28, 30
Internet, 55, 91
Investigation agents, 89
Irish Catholics, 25

Jackson, Janet, 17
Jemison, Mae C., 145
Jews, 27, 31, 46
Jim Crow laws, 29
Job security, 99
Johnson, Lyndon, 38
Joint Chiefs of Staff, 9, 130

Kerner Commission, 38
Khran, 28
King, Jr., Dr. Martin Luther,
  24, 109, 144, 148
Know-Nothings, 24-25

Lee, Spike, 24, 62
Library, 67, 89-90, 133,
  147
  cataloging systems, 89
  staff, 66, 90
Locke, John, 16
Love, 78, 85
  for self, 44

Magna cum laude, 2
Maltz, Maxwell, 37
Masculinity, 21
Maslow, Abraham, 71, 72
Massacre, 28
  Wounded Knee, 25
Mate, 81

Index

Media, 33-40
Million Man March, 146
Minorities, 3 ,33, 35, 98
Modem, 89
Morrison, Toni, 145
Moseley, Carol, 145
Motivation, 129-39
Murder rates, 3
Music, 88, 133

National Advisory
    Commission on Civil
    Disorders, 38
National Football League
    (NFL), 144
National Guardsmen, 142
Native Americans, 25, 98, 107
Nazis, 27
Necessities, 53
Needs, 53
Negative, 118
    ideas, 37
    people, 82-85
Networking, 101
Note taking, 105

Obstacles, 63, 123
    mental, 44
Oligarchy, 28
Opportunities, 142
Overboard, 19

Parkinson, professor
    Northcote, 111
Patronize, 47

Pavlov, Ivan, 119-20
Peers, 6, 13, 17, 130
People, 4, 23, 31, 36, 59, 67,
    90, 115, 141
    positive, 132-33
    negative, 82-85
    successful, 59
Perceptions, 36
Personality, 16, 71, 117
Pessimism, 83
Philanthropist, 9
Pink slip, 96
Places of interest, 134
Plantation, 18
Play, 114
Politicians, 45, 75, 78, 149
Polygraph, 75
Post slavery, 20
Poverty, 11, 17, 66
    black children, 3
Powell, Colin, 9, 130
Power, 144, 145
    personal, 142
Prejudice, 12, 40, 43, 74, 98,
    150
Prison, 3, 6
Prisoners of war (POWs), 17
Process, 59
Procrastination, 111, 115, 124,
    132
Projects, 148
Psycho-Cybernetics, 37

Questions, asking, 103
Quotas, 98

170 *The Color of Racism*

The Color of Racism
is the new way to easily
overcome discrimination!

Autographed copies of *The Color of Racism* will make perfect gifts for those you care about.

To place your order, complete the following information and mail to the address below.

1. Yes! Please send me _____ copies of *The Color of Racism*, autographed by the author, Sam B. Pearson, III, to each of the following persons:

   I. _____

   II. _____

   III. _____

   *If you need more room, use a separate sheet.

2. Enclose check or money order payable toTransformax Books for the appropriate amount ($12.95 plus $1.50 for shipping and handling, per book). Please do not send cash. Allow up to three weeks for delivery.

3. Name _____

   Address _____

   City _____

   State/Zip _____

   Phone ( ) _____ – _____

4. Mail order to: **Transformax Books**
   701 Loyola Avenue
   P.O. Box 53082
   New Orleans, Louisiana 70153-3082

Cut along dotted lines ✂

The author, Sam B. Pearson, III, is available for:

- Autograph sessions

- Interviews

- keynote speeches and presentations

- Educational and motivational seminars on overcoming discrimination, improving race relations, and resolving conflicts, customized for companies, schools, and organizations.

For more information, write to:

Transformax International
701 Loyola Avenue
P.O. Box 53082
New Orleans, Louisiana 70153-3082

Or, call :
(800) 655-7388 Monday to Friday, 9:00 a.m. - 5:00 p.m. Central Time